RAAW

RAAW

Rediscovering African American
Wisdom

Joseph William Shorter III

iUniverse, Inc.
New York Lincoln Shanghai

RAAW
Rediscovering African American Wisdom

iUniverse books may be ordered through booksellers or by contacting:

iUniverse
2021 Pine Lake Road, Suite 100
Lincoln, NE 68512
www.iuniverse.com
1-800-Authors (1-800-288-4677)

Because of the dynamic nature of the Internet, any Web addresses or links contained in this book may have changed since publication and may no longer be valid.

ISBN: 978-0-595-40702-6 (pbk)
ISBN: 978-0-595-85066-2 (ebk)

Printed in the United States of America

RAAW
Rediscovering African American Wisdom

iUniverse books may be ordered through booksellers or by contacting:

iUniverse
2021 Pine Lake Road, Suite 100
Lincoln, NE 68512
www.iuniverse.com
1-800-Authors (1-800-288-4677)

Because of the dynamic nature of the Internet, any Web addresses or links contained in this book may have changed since publication and may no longer be valid.

ISBN: 978-0-595-40702-6 (pbk)
ISBN: 978-0-595-85066-2 (ebk)

Printed in the United States of America

RAAW

Rediscovering African American Wisdom

Joseph William Shorter III

iUniverse, Inc.
New York Lincoln Shanghai

This book is dedicated to the countless individuals who have poured into my life, whether they know it or not. Listed in no particular order:

Jesus Christ, my Lord and Savior
Thank you for dying for my sins, conquering death, and showing me true love.

Laura H. Shorter, my mother
You showed me what true strength is while teaching me how to care. Your example of a strong woman has shaped my life. Thanks you for being just who you are. I thank God that you are my mother.

Joseph W. Shorter II, my father
Dad, I am so glad that I know you and have a relationship with you today. There are so many stories of anger and hate from children to fathers. I would like you to know that I love you and I see so much of you in me.

Mrs. Nicks—High School Teacher
Mrs. Nicks, you will forever live in my heart. You were my mother when I was at school and you loved and cared for me like I was yours. Thanks you for the support at my graduation, your love held me up.

Miquiel L. Banks, friend
My longest and craziest friend. I have and continue to enjoy the intelligent and intellectual conversations. It is rare that one person can share so many stories with another person full of adventure. You are like a brother.

David A. Cross, friend
You saw in me more than the homeless kid living in a brokendown car with no heat. Your kindness offered me a place to rest my head and my life has never been the same since. You showed me that we are our brother's keeper.

Jasmine Shorter, daughter
You are the sweetest little girl on the planet and I am proud that you call me daddy. I am excited to see all the ways you will impact this world. I love you sweetheart.

Ndubisi Nwachuku, friend
My Marine Corps brother, friend, and confidant. You helped me learn about leadership in a hostel environment. Some people are just "cool". It is good to know that someone always has your back.

Ms. Constance S. Blaize, wife and best friend
I can't even begin to tell you how much I love you. Throughout our friendship, I never thought we would be married. It is awesome being married to your best friend and my life is so much brighter with you in it as my wife. I LOVE YOU SO MUCH!

"It is not enough to know there can be no left without the right or no joy without pain, but we must experience our failures for God to build our successes."
By: *Joseph Shorter,*

"It is not enough to know there can be no left without the right or no joy without pain, but we must experience our failures for God to build our successes."
By: *Joseph Shorter,*

Contents

Preface xiii

Introduction xv

CHAPTER 1 Understanding Your Anger 1

Five Minutes 3

Ebony Pearl 6

CHAPTER 2 You Don't Have To Remain A Victim 10

Why Does the Free Man Scream? 11

Conditioning 11

Playing the Victim 16

Relationships 17

For Her (Man to Woman) 17

For Him (Man to Man) 20

CHAPTER 3 Taking Responsibility for Your Life and
Decisions 22

Our Thinking 25

Hit the Clock 25

Informed? 29

Pop Quiz 29

CHAPTER 4 The 'Faces' of Life 31

Emotional 31

Physical 33

Guys 33

Women 34

Intellectual 36

Spiritual. 37

Powerful Me 38

Scenario. 39

God's Way. 40

CHAPTER 5   Self-Profiling 42

Intrapersonal Examination. 42

Self-Righteousness 43

Exercise 1. 44

Living in Three Dimensions 45

Exercise 2. 46

Exercise 3. 46

Exercise 4. 46

CHAPTER 6   The Emotional Underverse 47

How do we cope?. 50

GOD Is There. 51

CHAPTER 7   Walking in Power 53

Identifying Sources of Power 53

Friends. 53

"The best thing a Friend can be is Available" 54

Community. 54

Talking the Talk 55

Walking the Walk 56

Conclusion 59

Resources, Research & Suggested Readings 61

Answers to Pop Quiz. 63

About The Author. 67

Preface

This book will explore the lives and attitudes of men and women in America. This book is written by an African American male, and so its point of view is unique in that regard. However, information and suggestions contained within are not necessarily specific to African American males. This work attempts to deal with issues that are common to most Americans, although some are specific to African Americans. Many people who read these pages might find this point of view new and refreshing, direct and enlightening. Take from it what you will, knowing that its purpose is to stir your thoughts and emotions, as well as to motivate each of us to more productive and positive lives.

Introduction

I am a Christian, so my perspectives are from a Christian point of view. Of course, this alone doesn't ensure credibility to the world at large does it? Gandhi, one of the most celebrated activists the world has ever seen, could not see the benefits of being a Christian when he compared our talk with our walk. The principles we claim as Christian are the very principles by which he lived his life, yet Gandhi never accepted Christ as his savior. There are others, like the Dalai Lama, whose spirituality is unquestioned by most people, and he is a Buddhist. (By the way, Buddha means "Awakened One," referring to a person who has obtained enlightenment, not to a person who is God incarnate.) For the purposes of this book, I am going to exclude the many religions that are not monotheistic. However, whatever your faith (and there are over three hundred of them worldwide), it probably encompasses the same basic principles that lead us to live our lives productively. Although practices and rituals can greatly differ, we all are seeking the same thing—God, or to be closer to him. For me, God is to be found through Christ Jesus, his only begotten son. I certainly encourage anyone who is not a Christian to find out for themselves what the religion is all about. However, regardless of your faith, there is power in the overriding principles that many religions teach. If you can draw from the strength in these teachings, they will help you become a better person and citizen of the world.

I find myself at an interesting crossroads. When I look back, I am thankful for what God has done for me despite myself. And yet, I am terribly disturbed by what I have *not* done in thirty-two years of life. Like so many African Americans, I realize that the illusion of success has fueled my apathy.

I discovered that my daughter Jasmine cannot read. After a two-week stay during the summer, it became apparent that my five-year-old was already behind academically. This discovery was particularly painful because I already feel that we, as African Americans, generally have more obstacles to overcome to begin with. I struggled to balance my disappointment with trying to be a source of encouragement to her. Since Jasmine lives with her mother hundreds of miles away, I feel handicapped, and I am angry that her mother has allowed this to happen.

This situation set me on a path of revelation that would only be made clear after I discovered a book titled *Black Heroes* by Jesse Carney Smith. Before I discuss how this book "stirred up" my emotions and helped me to reestablish some personal goals, let me give you some particulars about the book. It is a collection biographies of African Americans whose lives have had a significant impact on the world at large. It includes painters, poets, musicians, singers, actors, athletes, United Nations representatives, and heads of state, and impressive amounts of history are captured between its covers.

I am disturbed by my own lack of achievement but encouraged that God has not abandoned an unworthy son. My distress comes chiefly from the fact that, until recently, I have not been an avid reader. Sure, I could point to my dyslexia—a condition that has affected my desire to read—but that would serve only as an excuse for my underachievement.

Furthermore, I know very little of my African culture or the contributions of African Americans during the past four hundred years. This admitted ignorance leads me to the conclusion that I am severely ill-equipped to pass on this heritage to a younger generation—one that is in such desperate need of it. If I know little about the talents, the diversity, the intelligence, and the awe-inspiring achievements of those who have gone before and paved the way, how, then, can I pick up where they have left off? This revelation came to me in the only way possible in today's segregated America—through reading.

And so, I have started reading about the lives and achievements of African Americans, and, in short, their stories are inspirational. Most of the people I have read about so far were instrumental in the Harlem Renaissance, a time in beginning in the 1920s when African American art, music, dance, and social commentary began to flourish in a particular section of New Your City called Harlem., and the sheer talent and depth of these African Americans are astounding. However, the pride that swells my chest is quickly followed by an overwhelming wave of horror and despair. It has been said, "If you want to hide anything from a black man, put it in a book!" I am not sure who coined this phrase, but I *am* sure that, despite its racist undertones, it has indeed applied to me for thirty years. It applies, however, no longer.

If I have been deprived by myself and others of such powerful and inspiring information, then of what have African Americans, as a people, been deprived? I see constantly unrealized potential in myself, my ex-wife, family members, church members, co-workers ... the list goes on. The great gifts that were used by the trailblazers lie in each of us, but our laziness has kept us from fulfilling our potential.

I have been blessed with many talents, but when I consider what little I have done with them, it is quite disconcerting. I have gotten through life using my above-average intelligence, a strong work ethic, and, most of all, God's grace. In August of 2002, these advantages allowed me to purchase my first house. Occasionally, I would pat myself on the back for escaping from an incredibly hard childhood riddled with abuse and dysfunction to a middle-class black America. I would fool myself into thinking that I had "arrived." However, God has a way of letting you know just how small you are, especially when you are able to see yourself from a different perspective. Throughout my life, I have had personal interactions with God in the form of conversations with angles, and these experiences are the basis for why I believe God exists. Moreover, these encounters have often been my motivation for change and action, prodding me to pursue my goals and dreams. Take this book, for instance—I believe that it was God-inspired. I believe that I received a providential nudge to motivate me toward reaching my potential. In short, I believe that this book is the result of God telling me to get off my butt and contribute more, do more, *be* more. And the first step toward these goals was putting down the remote control and picking up and reading as many books as I could..

In the couple of years since becoming a member of Bible-Based Fellowship Church in Tampa, Florida, I have been in the company of many Black heroes—pastors who have been invited to come and preach, most prominently Rev. Arthur T. Jones and his wife, Doris. The church hosts an annual week-long session called "Listening to the Elders," during which older, experienced, and decorated individuals discuss the current condition of the United States as it pertains to African Americans. The first year I attended, it hit me rather hard intellectually. While I didn't agree with every point that was made, it was clear that these people had spent a great part of their lives not only thinking about these things, but actively seeking to make an impact. This led me to ask myself what impact *I* was making. In fact, I began to wonder whether anyone out there was really doing anything to address the African American condition in America outside the walls of the church.

I have found that I am good at one thing in particular—talking about various subjects. However, I have come to realize that it is a struggle for me to *do* something about what I feel, rather than simply talking about it. I fear that we are producing more individuals who aren't actually *doing* anything about anything. As a matter of fact, many of us get all emotional and fired-up about what everyone else has done to contribute to our misery, but seldom do we do anything to overcome the situation. I am not sure at what point the gene to fight the status quo stopped being the dominant gene, but something has to be done.

For this reason, I have decided to not just exist as a man physically, but actually to become a "Man." I have come to the realization that becoming a Man is an ongoing process, simply because life is an ongoing process. If that is not confusing enough, consider that life has many "Faces," or common areas of life where we express our existence through outward interaction, that also require us to be a Man. Follow me as I attempt to explore American life from the unique perspective of a thirty something black male. I believe that my insights will have many benefits for anyone who decides to read this book and will certainly stimulate conversations about the topics discussed within.

Chapter 1

Understanding Your Anger

A black man's anger is a deep-seated impulse that began before our ancestors were forcibly removed from Africa to be slave labor. However, for the sake of discussion, let's begin at that time in history when we were herded across the Atlantic to the New World. Most black men, when we first become aware of the atrocities committed upon our forefathers, feel a sweeping anger, which tends to be followed by confusion. Sporadically, we are even filled with pride as we imagine the strength it must have taken to survive the hardships of the Middle Passage.

> The Middle Passage Atlantic slave trade
> The captives were about to embark on the infamous Middle Passage, so called because it was the middle leg of a three-part voyage—a voyage that began and ended in Europe. The first leg of the voyage carried a cargo that often included iron, cloth, brandy, firearms, and gunpowder. Upon landing on Africa's "slave coast," the cargo was exchanged for Africans. Fully loaded with its human cargo, the ship set sail for the Americas, where the slaves were exchanged for sugar, tobacco, or some other product. The final leg brought the ship back to Europe. ("Middle Passage," from PBS.org [**http://www.pbs.org/wgbh/aia/part1/1p277.html**])

However, that pride is again overwhelmed by the sheer horror of our recent history (the past four hundred years of servitude and ongoing struggle of equality). Consider how many of us learned about these things before we knew the name Dr. Martin Luther King Jr.? Moreover, if we think about it, just how much of our history is even in public-school textbooks? On a personal note, I never knew Martin Luther King Jr. even existed until I moved to Atlanta at the age of eleven. If this doesn't seem unusual, then you've just made my point; if it *does*, then, again, the point is clear. Of course, this is just the beginning of the underlying emotions of anger, because we soon learn about how Dr. King was murdered, as were other great black leaders, such as Malcolm X.

A tide of desire for retribution swells within us, and we want to lash out—but at whom? This is where things get confusing, because no one we know is responsible for what happened nearly forty years ago, let alone four hundred. In fact, America today, the non-minority portion, proclaims that racism doesn't exist in any significant form, and that, on the surface, it is hard to see. In fact, if you are not a person of color, to see racism does indeed require a hard look at society at large, because you are not the intended victim. It might even be worth asking yourself whether you are contributing unwittingly to the problem. Shockingly, one can even be African American and subconsciously contribute to the hidden racism that plagues us today; so, if you are a person of color, you are not off the hook either.

There are other issues that contribute heavily to our anger aside from how America at large looks at us in general. While I acknowledge that there are many well-adjusted African American families in this country who may not identify readily with what is about to be stated, there are many others who agree with my point of view all too readily.

Let's begin with the absent father. A father can be "absent" in a number of different ways. First, there is the literal meaning of absence, which stretches all the way back to the time when families were torn apart because of the booming slave trade in Africa. Consider how the Black Man was first forced to leave his family for various reasons, the most notable of which was being sold to another slave master. Unfortunately, this was just the beginning of a domino effect that has continued to affect the African American family to this very day. The father was stripped of his family and self-respect was beaten or tortured out of him, leaving mothers to perform fathers' roles in addition to their own.

So, let's fast forward to the point at which my personal experience picks up, with my own father. All fathers have been charged by nature to be the breadwinners of the family, but our country did everything it could to frustrate and degrade any effort by an African American man to be an adequate provider for his family. Even those who did find economic success were often emotional failures in a lot of key ways, and not without reason. For one, the black male found (and continues to find) himself battling a hostile world on every front. Just finding and keeping gainful employment was and still is difficult, at best.

Furthermore, after having to deal with everything the world threw at him daily, he would only return home to a different type of battleground. Unfortunately, women did not have it any easier. The same struggles that the father contended with also affected the Black Woman, but in a different way. The way she dealt with the dichotomy between loving and supporting her husband and the stresses of financial hardship were often seen by the husband as non-supportive. This perception tended to compound the man's unbearable shame of not doing better for his family. So, what should have been a safe haven turned into a scene of bitter rivalry. How did he respond? Often, he turned to alcohol, drugs, other women, and similar temporary refuges. All of these things were used in an attempt to fill a void. Of course, none of them can provide a lasting escape from the misery of reality. In fact, they only work to prevent us from reaching our potential. Our fathers felt alone in a world that hated, envied, and feared them. In my opinion, not much has changed.

Aside from ourselves, black women have the most to benefit by understanding the internal struggle that persists within us. We need our women in order to survive! We die a little every day in a world that doesn't seem to want us very much. How do we stay afloat? How can we be the Man we have the potential to be? While these are very deep and difficult questions to even attempt to answer, I offer the following poem to suggest a start:

Five Minutes

All I need is five minutes for a place to lay my head.
A quiet place of light and love instead.

I will give you all I have, if only you would let me hold you like a baby does his mother—for only 300 beats of your heart.
Then I can stop, refuel, and begin again to be that strong man you admire so much—if for me, you will only play this part.

I understand that you have things to share and concerns to bear.
I know and truly want to hear everything you have to say, but I ask, do you have five minutes first to spare?

You see, life seems so much like a freeway at rush hour, and soon the lights and sounds begin to blur.
In the madness, as we seek to silence the voices in our heads, we cling to that place, that space, just five minutes of her.

We are strong! Yes. Leap tall buildings in a single bound we could, hand the world to you on a silver platter we should.

We do have a weakness, though: a desire—no, a *need* to close our eyes and feel the soft skin of your bosom against our cheek, hearing nothing but the soft, assuring thump of your heartbeat.

Five minutes—that is the key to a hidden reservoir of strength, power, love, and passion.
Will you be my sanctuary, allow me to be vulnerable yet secure in your arms? Just five minutes—that is all I am asking.

—Joseph W. Shorter III
08/15/2005

As children, our perspectives are obviously very different. My personal experience plays out something like this:

What I saw as a young man in my own family was not only a father who was angry, but also one who didn't seem to care for me and my sisters, it seemed clear to me that he chose to make another family to forget how he failed us. To us, our mother was the most precious thing in the world, and he disrespected her, abused her verbally and physically, and then cast her and us aside like used cartons of milk.

I can also suggest what a young girl might have seen in such a situation. She would have seen, in addition to those things already stated, a mother who manipulated her father out of necessity, and so the young girl might well have learned this skill, while simultaneously learning to distrust men. These types of situations have been perpetuated for decades, and so it makes sense that most young men now are angry, but not quite sure why. Sure, some women may be the breadwinners of their families, and this particular dysfunctional structure might not apply to everyone. However, if we can identify the issues and recognize how complicated they truly are, we might reveal a path to understanding.

The easy thing to do would be to blame the "White Man" for all of our troubles. Of course, that blame isn't necessarily always misplaced, but fixing blame does nothing to heal. And besides, *which* white man? All of them? As a result of our confusion and blanket mistrust, we have made pimps, rappers, basketball players, musicians, actors, and the like into our heroes and role models. These individuals represent only a fraction of who we are and what we are capable of, and should not be our only examples for what a man should be, especially considering that only a handful of them seem to act very responsibly. Unfortunately, there aren't many role models that young black men can physically touch. A growing number of us are unable to look to our own fathers' examples, and this is the real crime. For proof, examine the most recent college enrollment statistics. There is also the fact that African American males are disproportionately represented in county, state, and federal correction facilities, which is a result of their inability to sort through their anger and navigate a hostile world. This leaves black women with few choices. Then, as if things weren't bad enough already, the coming out of the closet of the "down low brothers" makes finding a suitable companion even worse for our sisters. Yes, we are mad, and we have good reason to be. However, it is not our anger that is at issue—it is what we do about it, for ourselves, our sisters, and our futures.

In the preceding paragraphs, I took a moment to suggest to "our" women how they might help us sort out some of our anger and help channel it into something more positive. I would now like to take a moment to do the same from the opposite perspective. Fellas! We have to start treating our women better. How can a young girl experience the full potential of being a woman if we don't treat her mother like a lady? Do you think that women today are more confident and capable than they have ever seemed before? Wake up! They have *always* been capable but have been forced to suffer us tearing down their self-esteem in order to make ourselves feel superior. We should understand that how we treat our women directly affects how we prosper in the future as well as the quality of our lives in the present. We need to open the doors for our women—for *every* woman, for that matter! We need to show them the respect that is due them. Every woman that we cross paths with will take her experience of us with her into every aspect of her life. What a powerful opportunity we have as men to teach them to expect a certain level of treatment and to respect themselves. Instead, so many of us seem to focus on exploiting them. We don't have to rely on the "White Man" anymore to exploit our women; we have taken the challenge and are doing a stellar job! Again, this issue is not something you can just take a pill for, wait fifteen minutes, and expect to get all better. No, it will take time and determination over several generations to correct the behaviors that pervade our culture. However, it starts by changing how black men see black women to begin with. Men have to see them as more than just another sexual conquest or convenient punching bag for all that plagues them. Instead, we must aspire to see deeper into women's souls and to show them what we see. Here is another poem that might help me make my point:

Ebony Pearl

A precious gift to Man,
this woman and her dark tan.
A Goddess of the sea,
her beauty preserved eternally.

Her hips have the curve of the Nile,
and that walk gets attention for miles and miles.
When I see her I try not to stare,
but then I'm drawn to the flow of her hair.

In the middle of the night I awake to see,
her chest rise and fall as this angel sleeps.
She is a lover, a mother, and best friend.
I love the small of her back, the curve of her chin.

When she talks I am hopelessly lost in her charm,
the world around can no longer do me harm.
She doesn't just speak, rather subtly commands;
my heart is immediately put in her loving hands.

I gladly place all that I have at her feet,
The last image of my mind as I drift to sleep.
Nothing is too good for one such as this.
One kiss from her lips is the price of complete bliss.

A creature of virtue, a work of divine art,
this woman has intimate knowledge of the secrets in my heart
She is a lady of power; she makes men out of men.
She taught me how to love from beginning to end.

She was a jewel to behold even as a little girl,
I give my life, my love to her forever, this, my Ebony Pearl.

—Joseph W. Shorter III
11/17/1999

Once we establish in our minds and hearts that a woman is a precious jewel, we can then begin showing that respect outwardly by reflecting how honest we are with ourselves when dealing with them. What I mean is that we should search our hearts, minds, and desires to get a handle on what we want from every individual woman we are interacting with. The following questions are just a small sampling of the types we can consciously and intentionally ask ourselves:

- Are we looking for the comfort of sex?

- Is it friendship that most endears us to her?

- What is she looking for from me? Am I willing to give her that?

- Am I leading her on because she makes me feel wanted, even though I have no real intention of having a sustained intimate relationship?

Once we know the true answers to such questions, we can begin to determine whether our intentions are selfish and cruel or genuine and benign. You might ask why we can't just have fun and be adults about it. Well, we can. The problem is that pain and dysfunction aren't normally a result of our desires and intensions, but rather of our lack of honesty in communicating our desires and intentions. All of us have basic fundamental needs that extend beyond food, drink, and sleep. In fact, we have a deeper requirement to be fulfilled mentally, physically, and, most of all, spiritually than we are usually aware of. We actively and subconsciously seek to satisfy these needs through using the people around us. The need we feel to be a part of something larger and to be desired by others are acted out, often in very damaging behaviors. For example, some women are promiscuous because of this deep-seated desire to be desired. What do we men do to these women? Unfortunately, a great number of us exploit their vulnerability, then have the nerve to feel good about our conquests later. We are hardly even aware of the continual damage and anguish we are creating by our selfish behavior.

Ask yourself if this sounds like you: "I'm not exactly sure what I want for my future in a relationship. I'm currently dating a beautiful woman. I was into her when we first hooked up. Now, she seems a little clingy. Sure, I poured the romance on and swept her off her feet. In fact, I'm proud of and impressed with how suave I can be. Now, however, I think she wants more than I can give. She's inviting herself into places that, yeah, I invited her into at first—but doesn't she know that it was only a temporary pass? She really is cool, but this other honey I'm checking out is just what I'm looking for right now. Hmm … how do I slow things down with the current one to give myself space to pursue this new girl? In my head, I know that the current one seems like marriage material, but I'm not ready for that right now. Do I really want to give up my freedom? Man! This is too heavy; I just need some space."

If this seems way too familiar, then you need some help, my brother. First, such thoughts are signs of emotional immaturity, which is totally independent of your physical age. Unfortunately, men of all ages suffer from this, but there is hope. We should understand that relationships are about taking risks. We men are not big on taking emotional risks at all. But they are risks, however, that we must take! We (both men and women) can better our odds by being honest with each other, but mostly by being honest with ourselves. We need to figure out what non-physical characteristics attract us to another person. Inevitably, a person will seem less attractive as we become aware of more of their faults. I am referring to the ones that we all hide so well when we are dating. Keep in mind that, no matter how attractive anyone is, he or she surely has annoying faults too, so you shouldn't base your decision on outward beauty alone. More importantly, you must ask them the difficult questions that they quite likely have never really been asked. It would be a good idea for you to ask and answer these same questions for yourself before you ask them of someone else.

- Do you believe in God? Why? What makes him real to you?
- Are you a Democrat, Republican, Independent, or nothing? Why? Do you even vote?
- Are you pro-life? Why or why not?
- Do you exercise? What is your diet like?
- Are your parents still married?
- Did you have a happy or sad childhood? Why?
- Do you consider yourself "high maintenance?"
- Would you consider yourself financially responsible? Why or why not?
- How important is marriage to you at this stage of your life?
- What do you want from a relationship?
- What do you have to offer in a relationship?
- What do you like to do for fun?
- What would you do if neither money nor time were an issue?

- What is your greatest talent? What is your passion in life?
- Are you neat or sloppy when no one is watching?
- What is your view of sex before marriage?
- How many times have you truly been in love?

Actually, just asking yourself and answering the questions are not really enough. You should write down your answers in an essay format. Why? Because this will force you to explore your true opinions, and not those given to you by your parents, guardians, culture, or friends. This is how you can discover who you really are and what pushes your buttons. These are obviously just a few of the questions that can be asked—there are many, many more. You must also understand that your answers may change as you grow in experience and mature emotionally.

Now, then, we have a foundation that can be built on as we engage in a serious relationship. Guys, you need to fully understand what you are doing when you don't respect and protect women. Women, you should know that trust is something that a man will require from you—even though it may be difficult for you to give, your relationship will never reach its potential unless you risk trusting him. No, there is no guarantee that he won't violate your trust. However, he can't violate a trust that he doesn't truly have. If you don't let go of your fear of dishonesty, your efforts to keep him close will only succeed in driving him away.

What we can unleash within us is powerful, but that power can be positive or negative. We must try to continually be honest with each other. Men, make sure that you ask yourselves and your partners what you want out of the relationship (monthly, at least), so that maintaining the status quo becomes a conscious decision. So often, we believe that what our partners told us a month or even year ago remains valid today. The truth is that, as we grow and experience life, what we want from each other and from life often changes. I will touch on relationships throughout the remainder of the book, because we need each other to truly make strides in repairing generations of damage.

Chapter 2

You Don't Have To Remain
A Victim

We certainly didn't choose to be slaves, nor do we desire to be absent fathers, bad husbands, or unfaithful lovers. Our struggle has been, and continues to be, a hard one. We were and are victims of cruel individuals and institutions. You can't always control whether or not you will become a victim, but it is your choice to remain one. We have a responsibility to get up and get on with our lives—if not for ourselves, then for the generations to come. We all have sad stories to tell, but these stories are meant to be a testimonies to our journeys, not etchings on our tombstones. It is natural to experience self-loathing and depression when we have been traumatized—but then what? It is the child in us that settles into blaming everyone else for our lot in life, and it is easy to fixate on American history and the awful treatment we and our ancestors have suffered. Days, months, and years can go by in such misery without us accomplishing anything of value. Instead, we must become the ones who decide our own fate. We are a brilliant people that has relegated itself to servitude long after the literal slaves have been set free. Of course, I believe that recognizing and putting a face on our oppressors is important, but we can't let the problem dictate our response. Rather, we must let our response dictate our future.

"Don't let someone else define your future by pushing you down, and then accommodate them by not getting up."
From *The Ramblings of Joseph Shorter*
03/01/2005

POEM:

Why Does the Free Man Scream?

Why does the free man scream? Is it because his freedom is just an illusion, a dream? What is freedom, anyway? Just a way to remove all the excuses for our self-inflicted dismay? No longer is it chains that bind us, or the slave-master who grinds us. Rather, the choices we make—the steps our free legs take.

Why does the free man scream? Is it because his freedom is just an illusion, a dream? The bars are now hidden; traps we cannot see. We walk in willingly now, no more whips or beatings for encouragement. Now we run to our fate—sucking on lollipops knowing our teeth will rot.

Why does the free man scream? Is it because his freedom is just an illusion, a dream? How can we ever be free from the choices we make, the consequences we take? Why can't we just do this, or that, and run from our mistakes?

Why does the free man scream? Is it because his freedom is just an illusion, a dream? The world is a circle round for a reason of cosmic scale. You see, things are in a circle because what you send out will return. So be sure that you are not sending out your own personal hell.

The free man screams because he realizes that there is no freedom from the consequences of the choices he makes. There is only the promise that kindness may not be returned; love may not be everyone's concern. The hope is that he matters to someone, somewhere, and that eternity remembers his name.

—Joseph W. Shorter III
11/21/2005

Conditioning

Are you familiar with the concept of Pavlovian conditioning? Ivan Pavlov was the scientist who discovered the "conditioned reflex." He won the Nobel Prize in Physiology or Medicine in 1904. If you would like to know more about him, a simple internet search will generate a plethora of information. However, for the purposes of this book, let's concentrate on the crux of his discovery and how it relates to our subject. The following is a brief summary of Pavlov's discovery:

- Unconditioned stimulus (UCS)—stimulus that causes a natural response.
- Unconditioned response (UCR)—inborn reflex to a stimulus.
- Conditioned stimulus (CS)—a stimulus that causes a natural learned response due to association with a previous inbuilt response.
- Conditioned response (CR)—a natural learned reflex to a stimulus due to association with another inbuilt response.

Ref: http://en.wikipedia.org/wiki/Pavlovian_conditioning

Now that the scientific terms are out of the way, let me discuss the concept in a way that you can probably grasp.

Consider the following scenario:

You show someone a book and encourage them to pick it up and read it, but then ring a bell and hit their hand with a large stick every time they reach for it. What would happen? Likely, the person would build a conditioned response to not pick up the book. Eventually, you begin leaving the book in front of them when you are not in the room, but watching from a hidden location. They start reaching for the book, and, from your hiding place, you ring the bell! What do you think their response will be? They will probably draw back their hand abruptly in fear of punishment. If you do this for, say, four hundred years or so, you will probably never have to worry about that person learning to read, because they have been conditioned against it.

How can this conditioned behavior be unlearned? Well, over a period of time, you encourage the person to reach for the book. You continue to ring the bell when they do it, but, instead of punishing them, you reward them. Eventually, a new response is built. However, the memory of the old punishment will remain, and they will be ever wary of the day pain might follow the bell, instead of pleasure. In fact, you would probably need to pick the book up for them and put it into their hands repeatedly before beginning to regain trust.

Why did I take you through this scenario? So you can understand that we have developed learned responses that take time to overcome. However, I want to stress that the test subjects (us) need to have the courage and resilience to continue to reach for the book, even though it might be painful. This is what people like Gandhi, Martin Luther King Jr., Rosa Parks, and the countless other brothers and sisters of every race did for all of us. While these people did things on a cultural and socioeconomic level, our own learned behavior encompasses our very personal interactions with each other. When we abuse each other's trust, this behavior is perpetuated through generations to come. Instead of passing on the learned behavior of victims, we need to begin passing on the learned behavior of success, strength, and brilliance that lies within us all. We have a very rich inheritance that is hardly ever leveraged—our learned failure prevents it. We have to stop believing that we don't deserve to be happy. If we do find happiness, then we need to stop waiting for the other shoe to drop (like the return of the stick hitting our hands as we reach for new heights). The fact is, happiness is neither guaranteed nor something that can be given by someone else. We have to be active in making our lives positive and happy every day.

I feel obligated now to point out that Affirmative Action was, in my belief, created to combat this learned failure created by slavery and abuse in American history. I realize that many people have their own reasons to support or oppose Affirmative Action. Just keep in mind that even though no system is perfect (especially when administered or regulated by the federal government), having no system in place at all to attempt to redress this atrocity would be much worse. In fact, for America to wash its bloodstained hands of the matter would be a slap in the faces of every African American alive today and to those of the great leaders of the past who gave so much of themselves not just for equal rights, but also for equal opportunities.

It is natural (or is it learned?) and easy to concentrate on what depresses us. Have you ever wondered why the bad times in a relationship seem to dominate our memories instead of the positive times? We allow the negative situations in our lives to overshadow the positive much of the time. This is detrimental because it often hides opportunities that exist for us or lessons that should have been learned from the experience. It takes encouragement for us to see the positive side of the trials we go through, and it takes courage to do something with the knowledge that we have gained. We African Americans have got to change our responses to the curve balls life throws us. If you or someone you know recites one or more of the following phrases (or variations thereof) as a regular part of conversations with fellow sympathizers, then I am talking to you.

- "The Man" won't let me get ahead!
- I trained the white person to be my manager.
- They just don't want me to be in charge of them.
- I have to work twice as hard to earn less then they do.
- I keep bumping my head on the "glass ceiling."
- The "good-ole-boy" system is stifling my career growth in this company.

I am not suggesting that none of those statements can ever ring true in today's America. In fact, they can be quite accurate in many situations across this country. Furthermore, I am not suggesting that frustration and anger are inappropriate responses to such blatant racism. However, I do feel compelled to ask, "So what?" or, more accurately, "So what now?" We should be in touch with the barriers that we contend with daily; however, they should not imprison our minds and subsequently our being. No, in fact, we can use that suppression as motivation for us to build the energy we need to accomplish those things that we thought we could find only in our dreams. The truth is that we are all puppets in some sense. But are you going to let someone other than God lead and guide your actions? Deciding not to be a victim is a daily battle we all must fight. Sometimes, we may not win the battle—but it is important that we win the war.

Understand that there is no rule that says that you have to work for any company that seems to limit your career growth and opportunities. In fact, it might be that you have outgrown the company and the position that you hold. However, the boldness to take a chance and do something else is your burden alone. No one is going to call you up and say, "Hey! I have the perfect job for you, and it pays the salary and benefits you have always wanted, and more!" Forget it! You have to be willing to roll the dice from time to time. Of course, I am suggesting that you take a *calculated* risk. Don't throw caution to the wind and hope for God to figure it out for you! That is just bad decision-making. Let's be real and remember that there are probably other people who depend on us and our steady income. Remember, God gave you free will and the ability to make decisions for a reason. So, we must be smart, bold, and methodical on achieving your goals. First, we should make a habit of writing down what our goals are. I suggest dividing them into in minimum six-month increments, in order to have something clearly defined for specific stretches of time. Next, we should write down a summary action plan for achieving each goal. Here is a brief example:

Summary Action Plan

At the beginning of each week, I will spend a minimum of one hour writing down the goals that I reached and the ones I did not, in an effort to be more realistic and better set future tasks. At the end of the first month, I plan to have accomplished the following:

- List
- The proposed
- Accomplishments
- Here

Repeat this for every month, and then re-state the overall goal.

<u>We often trip ourselves up during the</u> weekly struggle to balance the scales of our lives. I find it amazing that we can be our own biggest critics, and yet, at the same time, be completely unwilling to acknowledge our own shortcomings even as we praise our strengths.

Of course, there are different types of personalities, and there are various ways in which we can victimize ourselves weekly, or even daily. I will just focus on the "Hard Worker"—that self-motivator. The Hard Worker is someone who seems perpetually busy. In fact, they are *always* busy. There are some decided advantages to this personality trait. They tend to be goal-oriented and have the potential to get many more tasks accomplished than others, in just as much time. They will jump right into the next task, moving straight onto the next thing in order to gain that ever-so-addictive feeling of accomplishment that only exists in the small window of reflection that opens immediately after tasks are completed. However, beware, they also feel frustrated, and even depressed, if goals are not completed within the allotted time. They often have too many balls in the air at once which ultimately serves to decrease overall efficiency. Unfortunately, depression can result if the number of incomplete tasks and goals grow beyond one's capacity to juggle them.

On the other hand, multi-tasking and a seemingly unlimited energy reservoir are major strengths if the person has vision and is relatively organized in their approach to and delegation of tasks. If they do not have vision or decent organizational skills, then they need to be partnered with someone who does. What does this have to do with "tripping ourselves up," you ask? Simply put, one can succumb to the tendency to forget to pencil any personal time into one's schedule.

As we go about seeking to achieve our personal goals, we have an elevated risk of workaholism which leads to unbalanced life. Therefore, it is not enough to have a plan, write it out, and methodically cross off task after task. You can achieve career or financial success without making overwhelming personal sacrifices. Unfortunately, we don't generally have a good sense of what our capacity is until we reach our limits, so we must be careful not to pile on obligations in our professional, social, and religious lives if we are uncertain that we can fulfill them comfortably. I suggest that you make a "to-do" list, check it twice, and force yourself to do something on that list weekly. I believe that this will help you considerably in avoiding the role of "victim."

Playing the Victim

I sit here wondering what is real; what tragedies, joy, pain, do these faces conceal? I know there is pain because of my own; I know there is joy or at least the hope of happiness; I know I am, because of these emotions and feelings that bombard my heart daily.

Why am I here? What do they want of me, beyond what is asked? How do I become the person so many think I already am? How do I become the person I wish I was? So many questions—but I can't seem to find the answers.

Where do I go from here? Is happiness just a dream dangled in front of me for the pleasure of some adversary I cannot see? The choices that present themselves seem too much to bear, but if I don't make any choice, then I have truly sealed my fate.

Why am I here? What do they want of me, beyond what is asked? How do I become the person so many think I already am? How do I become the person I wish I was? So many questions—but I can't seem to find the answers.

Do I stop and start all over, maybe? But how far can I run before the problems catch me again? Am I the problem? If so, then how do I escape myself? How do I fix—me? Maybe the responsible thing to do is to remove myself from society so that no one else gets hurt. Wouldn't that cause pain too?

Why am I here? What do they want of me, beyond what is asked? How do I become the person so many think I already am? How do I be the person I wish I was? So many questions—but I can't seem to find the answers.

—Joseph W. Shorter III
11/15/2005

Relationships

Ah, *love*! What a bittersweet taste you have! As I have indicated, we learn the basic skills of navigating a relationship from our parents (or whoever played that role). We often repeat our mistakes and carry them over from relationship to relationship, yet remain unable to figure out what dooms us to failure. We become victims of our own insanity, that seemingly uncontrollable urge to inflict misery on ourselves. A friend of mine (Dave Rabon) repeated an old saying, "The definition of insanity is to do the same thing over and over expecting different results." While this applies to much more than relationships, it certainly applies here. Believe it or not, we don't have to punish the next poor soul who decides to love us by making them responsible for every hurt and pain someone else has inflicted on us. Of course, *you* would never do that, right? Well, for those of us who aren't so well-adjusted, this is for you.

For Her (Man to Woman)

Although we sometimes pant, pee, and grunt like one, men are not dogs. If every man you meet tends to run away, it is possible that you might be guilty of some behavior that causes them to react this way. I know, ladies, this sounds like a biased perspective—it is. However, that doesn't make it useless; after all, it's us men whom you want to have a relationship with. Here are some common issues that seem to be just too much for us guys to deal with over the long haul:

1. Attempting behavior modifications? Stop it! You would hate it if we gave as much effort to this endeavor as you seem to.

2. Why is it that once the newness of the relationship wears off, we are no longer groomed to your satisfaction? Our nails are too dirty, our hair isn't cut often enough ... This was okay before we started dating.

3. For some reason, women seem to think that anything we give attention to, we like or love more than them. Understand that we need our own space and that this is not a threat to you.

4. Our mothers are not your competition. We desperately want you to love them as much as we do.

5. You don't have to be our virtual day-planner. This is a trick we play on you, although it turns out bad for us too. We are good at letting our women remember everything we are supposed to do. This is our way of dropping the burden of responsibility into your laps. Don't let us do it. We *can* remember perfectly well—we just choose not to.

6. A man probably has a different relationship with the remote control than you do. So do yourself and your man a favor, and recognize that you may not always be able to agree on what to watch. Establish the rules up front. We don't even channel-surf the same way a lot of the time. Trust me, understanding this will help more than you know.

7. Somehow, relationships seem to get to a point at which it feels like women are watching our every move—basically smothering us. Admittedly, we do this to you too, so it is something that both parties have to manage. Developing friends and activities of your own (*not* shopping) will help you to define yourselves, and this will help us learn how to better interact with each other.

8. Realize that our sense of time operates differently. When you say something like, "Will you take out the garbage?" understand that this does not translate to us as "Will you take out the garbage *now*?" This is as much a matter of miscommunication on your side as it is that, according to our system of prioritization, the particular task does not rank higher than surfing the ESPN channels. Yes, we will get to the trash—later. Of course, consistently forgetting to pick the baby up from day care is a different, more serious issue altogether.

9. Do not use sex and feminine wiles to manipulate us into getting or doing things. This basically makes you a very expensive call girl. This is not the same as role-playing and will only lead to trouble. Remember,

problems in the bedroom generally originate somewhere else. Find the source, and correct the issue there.

10. Men have varying levels of comfort with emotional availability, but this is directly affected by you. When we feel as though you are more concerned about us and less critical of everything we do, we will be more likely to open up to you. Understand that we need your support, not disapproval (no matter how subtle). You didn't hook up with the perfect guy. And guess what—we didn't hook up with the perfect woman, either.

11. Respect and understand limits. Yes, there are such things. You are very detailed by nature and want to describe all the garnish on the plate. We, however, first want to know whether there is steak on the plate. If you say too much without getting to the meat of the conversation, you begin sounding like Charlie Brown's schoolteacher. The only way to shock us back to attention once that happens is to say something like, "I'm pregnant." You will find that if you give us the meat quickly we will be more receptive to the garnish later.

Ladies, please understand that, our rough exteriors notwithstanding, many men are helpless, fragile little boys who crave your love and need to know that you desire us despite our vulgarities. We want more than anything to feel free to expose our weaknesses in an emotional refuge. Sounds dopey, huh? Well, maybe—but it's true. Consider the movie *King Kong* (the 2005 theatrical release), for example. Thanks to the wonders of computer-generated imagery, it is easy to identify with, and even empathize with, Kong's emotions. However, what stands out most are the primal emotions passing between Kong, Ann Darrow, and Jack Driscoll. Kong demonstrates very well a man's protective, strong, and monstrous outside, but he also shows us the infant-like vulnerability that exists in all men. Ann, of course, is portrayed as the typical woman: soft, beautiful, caring, and in touch with all of Kong's competing dynamics. Keep in mind that Kong's love is not sexual in nature, but rather closer to that of a best friend or child. It says, "You are beautiful, yes, but nurture me, love me, be available for me." Ann and Jack Driscoll, however, share a romantic love that motivates him to put his life at risk to rescue her. In reality, Kong and Jack Driscoll are the same person; they are every man. We want a woman who can recognize all of these aspects within us and nurture each one completely. It is also important to point out that Ann is not just a helpless nurturer; she is also strong, smart, resourceful, and self-sufficient.

In fact, she comes from a background that makes it clear that she is tough and independent. We, I suspect, male and female, want desperately to believe that this kind of selfless love not only exists, but is obtainable.

For Him (Man to Man)

Guys, a woman is not simply a conquest waiting to be had, although they certainly are a beautiful treasure. We have to begin thinking of women as much more than something to use up and toss away when we are no longer infatuated with them. A woman can be our greatest source of inspiration; she is often what motivates us to better ourselves and achieve greater goals. If you are a love-'em-and-leave-'em kind of guy, then check yourself, because you are wrecking much more than you know. Here are some things that you must learn in regards to how you interact with women:

1. Open doors for *all* women (repeat for memorization, bub). Of course, you should already know this. If she is the independent type, or is offended by your gesture, use some of that charm you claim to possess. Explain that your opening the door for her is not a statement of her inferiority or helplessness, but rather an honor that she is due, that this is your way of showing her and everyone else how elegant she is. Remember, chivalry is worthless if you are only trying to impress her. You must first believe in it yourself, or she will see through the charade.

2. Don't ever compromise your manhood to appease her mood swings. If you do, get ready for the ensuing frustration of trying to regain her respect. Women do like a man who is in touch with his feminine side, a man who hears her. However, she wants a *man*—someone who will stand his ground and not give in to her every whim. In my experience even the most independent woman wants this, despite all of the outward games that are played.

3. Pay more attention to your own grooming. Yes, I know that I got on women earlier for forcing this on us, but, honestly, they shouldn't have to. Here are some tips: trim and clean your nails, polish your shoes, comb your hair, and shave regularly. Remember that splashing on some cologne does not excuse you from bathing! Recognize that you may be a victim of chronic halitosis, and deal with it. Basically, try to develop grooming habits and rituals that become second nature.

4. We get on women a lot about body parts spreading, sagging, and, well … increasing. I myself am a pain in that I want to be physically attracted to the same woman I started dating some time ago. However, women cannot stop time (and neither can you), so don't expect them to be preserved like photos taken in their twenties. What we can do is encourage and express to them, as gently as possible, what is healthy. Of course, this means that you too have to get serious about your own fitness. Be an example, if this is important to you, and get rid of that beer gut!

5. Make sure that you are going somewhere. One of the saddest things to see is a grown man who still doesn't know what he wants to be when he grows up. What's even worse is a grown man who doesn't even have any motivation to be or do anything more than what he already is and does. Forget about what she thinks! Where is your self-respect, man? Apathy is our greatest enemy. Not only does it make us unsuitable for healthy long-term relationships, it also perpetuates a low standard of achievement that simply must stop.

Now, for both men and women, what does this relationship discussion have to do with realizing that we don't have to be the victim? Well, it's simple: once we get a handle on the things that cause us to repeat the mistakes from previous relationships, we become empowered to stop wallowing in self-inflicted misery. We also become better-prepared to deal with things like codependency issues. It is easy, and quite common, to blame the opposite sex for our social dysfunctions. While this provides ample material for a pity party, it does nothing to help us learn from our mistakes and move on to healthier relationships. So, educate yourself about yourself, and make this a continual pursuit.

Chapter 3

Taking Responsibility for Your Life and Decisions

Historical Note

Slavery in North America

Is not the slave trade entirely at war with the heart of man? And surely that which is begun by breaking down the barriers of virtue, involves in its continuance destruction to every principle, and buries all sentiments in ruin! When you make men slaves, you ... compel them to live with you in a state of war.
—Olaudah Equiano, former slave

Slavery became a highly profitable system for white plantation owners in the colonial South. In South Carolina, successful slave owners, such as the Middleton family from Barbados, established a system of full-blown, Caribbean-style slavery. The Middletons settled on land near Charleston, Carolina's main port and slave-trading capital. They took advantage of the fact that at the end of the 17th century, some of the earliest African arrivals had shown English settlers how rice could be grown in the swampy coastal environment. With cheap and permanent workers available in the form of slaves, plantation owners realized this strange new crop could make them rich.

As rice boomed, land owners found the need to import more African slaves to clear the swamps where the rice was grown and to cultivate the crop. Many of the Africans knew how to grow and cultivate the crop, which was alien to Europeans. By 1710, scarcely 15 years after rice came to Carolina, Africans began to out-number Europeans in South Carolina. • Arthur Middleton
• Harvesting the Rice

Slavery was rapidly becoming an entrenched institution in American society, but it took brutal force to imposed this sort of mass exploitation upon once-free people. As Equiano wrote, white and black lived together "in a state of war." The more harshly whites enforced racial enslavement, the more they came to fear black uprisings. As they became more fearful, they responded by further tightening the screws of oppression.

"If you're a white authority,
you're constantly trying
to figure how tightly you
want to impose the lid
with respect to people
running away. How fierce
should the punishments be?
Should it be a whipping?
Should it be the loss of a
finger or a hand or a foot?
Should it be wearing
shackles perpetually?"
—Peter Wood, historian

Carolina authorities developed laws to keep the African American population under control. Whipping, branding, dismembering, castrating, or killing a slave were legal under many circumstances. Freedom of movement, to assemble at a funeral, to earn money, even to learn to read and write, became outlawed.

Source:
http://www.pbs.org/wgbh/aia/part1/1narr5.html

The problem of low self-worth is not specific to any racial group in America. I am, however, speaking from an African American perspective. Our unique history in this country has facilitated a deep-rooted sense of defeat in us. We have a great ability to kill our own dreams by highlighting all of the barriers of the past and present. Many of us have become afraid of taking a chance and taking control of our own destinies. As I mentioned earlier, we often blame "The Man" or some other intangible person or group for all of our misfortunes in life. We are prone to suspicion of the government and to believing in conspiracy theories (sometimes with good reason, I might add) that deepen our mistrust of the very society we live in.

Now, before you assume that I am discounting these thoughts and emotions, understand that I have not mentioned any perspective so far that does not have merit. It is a fact that Africans were brought forcibly to this country as slave laborers. It is a fact that we have been the victims of government-sanctioned experiments and atrocities. (Read or watch the documentary about the Tuskegee experiment.) It is a fact that we have been mistreated, degraded, and underpaid since we first arrived in this country. It was a fact that government census was required when we were lynched while slavery was still legal, and it was not considered murder, or even recognized as such by the highest level of government, until relatively recently. If this seems outrageous to you, then I suggest that you do some research. I could go on and on, infinitely pointing out situation after situation that has conditioned us to the behavior that stunts our growth in the present-day America. I have included and excerpt from of an article from the Atlanta Daily Word website. Read the full article where the U.S. Senate apologizes for inaction on lynching between the years of 1882 through 1868.

WASHINGTON—The United States Senate formally apologized recently for its refusal to approve any of the 200 anti-lynching legislation bills introduced during the first half of the 20th century, a failure that led to the deaths of at least several thousand African-Americans.

During that period, the House of Representatives passed three anti-lynching measures but the Senate, controlled by powerful, Southern segregationists, never approved an anti-lynching bill.

Sen. George Allen (R-Va.), co-sponsor of the bi-partisan resolution with Sen. Mary Landrieu, (D-La.), said the resolution addresses what had been "a stain on the institution of the Senate."

Source:
http://www.zwire.com/site/news.cfm?newsid=14789445&BRD=1077&PAG=461&dept_id=237827&rfi=6

The good news is that history also shows that we are an incredibly resilient people. A deep faith in a higher power (God and Jesus Christ, usually) has fueled our people's resolve and kept lit the fiery flame of freedom. It gave uncommon people the uncommon valor to risk their lives and take the chances that have allowed us to enjoy the freedoms and incomes that so many of us earn today. Every road-block that was meant to destroy us has been overcome by faith and unmatched sacrifice. Those hard times of back-breaking hours in the cotton fields, and even the betrayal of one of us by another, gave us the strength we needed to survive. Unfortunately, some of the psychological remnants from a time not so long ago still shape our thinking today.

Our Thinking

What is it about our thinking that continues to enslave us? I'm sure that you've heard countless poems talking about a slavery of the body having been exchanged for shackles that imprison our minds—inspirational poems calling for black men and women to rise or get up and be counted in some fashion. It used to be that you would only hear poems of this kind recited at spoken-word sessions in local bookstores and cafés, but not anymore. We have now gone mainstream with the artistic expression of our plight. *Russell Simmons Presents Def Poetry* on HBO is a series that gives a much larger voice to this art form. No longer is it just a grass-roots movement.

POEM:

Hit the Clock

Brring! Brring! My brotha, get up! Bring! Bring! My brotha, get up!
Waste no time 'cause time cost paper,
Bring! Bring! Go run yo next big caper!

Brring! Brring! My brotha, get up I said!
What'cha think, someone is gonna just let you get ahead?
You heard the rumor, didn't you, bro?
They said we are naturally retarded—born slow.

Inferior, they scream; inferior, they sing,
We go out and prove it by chasing the hollow bling-bling!
Hollow inside, hollow upstairs; hollow-point slugs
Ain't nothing but dreams in hollow thug heads.

Bring! Bring! My brotha, get up, I said!
We are your ancestors wondering where their legacy has been hid.

We used to boast of Egyptian Sphinx and pyramids,
Now we disrespect our women and wear backward lids.
Disappoint us, disappoint you, disappoint me—disappointing youth.

Bring! Bring! My brotha, get up! Bring! Bring! My brotha, get up!
Remove the chains from your head; be a fool no more.
Show the world what lies inside that hidden treasure store.

One day we will shine, and that day is now.
Stop hustling to get by, watching the clock tick down.
Yeah, my brotha, hit the clock; get up and live the destiny, you can do it!
Get up, take a shower, get your mind right—just do it!

—Joseph William Shorter III
01/05/2006

"While we don't often choose to be a victim, we do often choose to remain one."
From *The Ramblings of Joseph Shorter*
03/01/2005

Get the point? Again, of all the people in the known history of the world (save the Native American indians), none have suffered the oppression and suppression experienced by African Americans. You may think this point is up for debate, but I would challenge anyone to find another people in history that can say it has endured over four hundred years of bondage and lost more lives, and still struggles in that same land for equality today. Keep in mind that we have also fought in every major war to earn our place in "The Land of the Free," yet still the struggle continues. The bonds that must now be broken are not made of steel, but of grey matter.

Note:
Native American Indians have certainly endured a similar oppression and remaining tribes today suffer from America's amnesia. To read more about this tragedy, do a simple google search: http://www.google.com/search?sourceid= navclient&ie=UTF-8&rlz=1T4GGLR_enUS211US211&q=The+Genocide+of+ Native+American+Indians

It all becomes a matter of choice. This sounds simplistic, I know, but it essentially boils down to choice. This choice, however, is one that we don't seem capable of making without a certain level of maturity and self-awareness. You see, there is no magic age at which some imbedded chemical process takes over and propels us into maturity. Furthermore, increased maturity alone is not enough. Self-awareness must also grow and mature to the point at which we are forced to ask ourselves basic questions about who we are and what our purpose is. Eventually, they begin to stitch together the intricate weave needed to replace our childhood blankie. Some of us do a whole lot better than others in this regard, which is evidenced by the enormous number of middle-aged fools with no pension, no desire, no healthcare, and no point. This may sound harsh, but you must understand that I am not referring to those individuals and families who are genuinely stricken by circumstance, nor our forgotten and helpless seniors. No, I refer to those people—like some of my own family members, I'm sorry to say—who live most of their lives in jail or running from the threat of it, refuse to go straight, have no plan for retirement, nor any desire to pass on anything more than debt.

Let us not forget our youth and young adults either—a group that is full of controversy and divisiveness We have so confused them that nothing seems sacred to them anymore. It seems that so many parents have chosen to lay down and make a baby, while all but stepping away from choosing to raise them. It is too inconvenient to be a parent these days, what with all the activities and time a child requires. Our kids are even taking clues from us and having their own babies while they are little more than infants themselves. Parenting is exhausting, yes, but if you are going to be irresponsible enough to have children, then at least be responsible enough to be involved in their rearing! If you are a parent (and the child lives with you), ask yourself these questions:

- Do I know the names of all my child's friends' parents?

- Do I have updated contact information for these children and parents?

- Do I have an up-to-date photo of my child?

- Do I make my child feel guilty about being involved in activities because I don't want to be bothered taking them and picking them up? Or do I make some other parent responsible for transporting my child to the events I should be attending?

- Do I respect my child's privacy, even though they don't pay a cent in rent? (Privacy is for people who pay rent or have mortgages).

- Does my child address adults as "sir" and "ma'am?"

- Do I monitor my child's schoolwork and grades?

- Do I allow my child to spend 90 percent of free time playing video games or talking on the phone?
- Does my child have a cell-phone bill larger than my own?

In truth, there are many things parents should be doing, but don't. As a result, our kids seem to be struggling more than ever to find their identities. They have chosen to make pimps, rappers, and professional athletes their heroes because we have failed to act heroically ourselves. Whatever happened to the days when kids dreamed of being astronauts, doctors, lawyers, and the like? Of course, some still do have such goals; I just fear that not enough of them do. Consider the low number of African American doctors, in any field, we have today. There are fewer African American males even choosing college anymore. I should mention that the number of college-bound African American females seems to be on the rise. The trend for males, however, is woefully evident at my own church, where there is a great disparity between the numbers of scholarships awarded to male and female recipients. Simply put, we have to give our youth more positive choices by getting involved in their lives. Checkout the link below for more information:

Source: http://www.census.gov/population/www/socdemo/school/cps2005.html

For the purposes of his discussion, young adults are those who fall between the ages of twenty-five and fourty-four. This group has enjoyed the benefits of the hard work and sacrifices of its grandparents and parents. This group also enjoys the largest income of all age groups combined. (see the source cited below) Yet, at least in my church, we seem to be the least involved in anything—especially tithing. We choose to rely on the very school system that we now know did an awful job with us; not only do we fail to help educate our kids, but we want our schools to raise them, too! What happened? What did our parents do to instill such apathy, selfishness, and greed in us? Oh, we know how to earn a buck, get an education, and pursue a career, but what about everything else? We have chosen *ourselves* over everyone and everything else. Young adults are also the most isolated among us. We drive expensive cars, buy expensive houses in gated communities, live there for years, and barely get to know our neighbors. The easy road seems to be our preferred path, and yet we wonder what's wrong with our kids. *We* are what's wrong with our kids—but we have the power to change this sad fact. If the kids truly are our future, what present, then—what legacy—are we going to give them to build upon? We stand on the shoulders of giants, and our children should stand even higher. Ask yourself whether you are making a significant (at least weekly) impact on any child. If the answer is no, then shame on you! Decide to change that about yourself today.

Source: http://pubdb3.census.gov/macro/032006/perinc/new09_000.htm

Informed?

This one is going to hit a lot of us right dead center. Not only do many of us have a poor knowledge of the history of this country (or any other), a lot of us don't have a clue about what is going on in the world today. This is not a "black thing," by the way—it is an American thing. It is our responsibility to be knowledgeable about the world we live in. The Jewish community, more often than most, makes it a point to educate its children about its collective history and to teach them to speak their ancestral language. We can learn from their example. Take this quiz and see how you do:

Pop Quiz

1. Without looking them up, write down the Ten Commandments.

2. What is the capital of the state that you live in right now?

3. What countries border Iraq?

4. Name ten countries in Africa

5. Name five significant black heroes, aside from Martin Luther King Jr., Malcolm X, and Frederick Douglass.

6. Without looking it up, what is the Fifteenth Amendment to the U.S. Constitution about?

7. Do you have a family tree? Yes or No.

8. What part of the country is Wyoming in?

9. Who was the sixteenth president of the United States?

10. Name three influential people of the Harlem Renaissance.

Okay, how did you do? I could offer up a scale ranging from poor to excellent, but the fact is that you and I should know the answers by heart—all of them! It's a sad fact that in this great country, we can even choose to be stupid every day.

Instead, let's choose to *learn* something daily and share that knowledge with someone else in addition to our kids. With all the ways we can instantly communicate these days, this shouldn't be difficult. One last thing—make it a practice to use multiple sources of news to include non-American sources as well; so that you are up to date on current events and can talk intelligently about the weighty subjects that your and someone else's child might be confused about. You might be surprised what happens if you have deep conversations with your kids from time to time.

Chapter 4
The 'Faces' of Life

In this chapter, I want to discuss the "Faces" of life that we live in. This is an abstract concept that will help to explain the common ways in which we all approach the everyday. Through these analogies, we can begin to understand our responses to people and situations, and, more importantly, begin to modify our own behavior so that it brings about more positive reactions.

Emotional

This is the most volatile Face that we have, and the one in which we spend most of our time. Unfortunately, a lot of major decisions in life are based on emotions, while excluding the logical and spiritual perspectives that could save us (and others) a lot of heartache. We all tend to be ruled primarily by our emotions, and, frankly, sometimes this has its strengths. We (African Americans) are an emotionally dramatic people. Our art, in its truest sense, is born out of our deep connection to our emotions. Consider how talented visually, poetically, and dramatically a people we are. No one could argue that we have not produced artistic giants across the planet. Furthermore, let us not forget that it is our emotions that connect us to all of the other Faces of life. Without emotion, we lose our connection to humanity, and it is our humanity, our sense of self-consciousness after all, that really makes us different from all of the other beasts that roam the planet. However, emotions unchecked can lead to disaster. We must be careful to maintain a delicate balance between our different Faces. Simply because, when we are emotional, we are more prone to do and say things we will regret, we should wait until cooler heads can prevail. Unfortunately, more times than not, the damage is too severe to salvage later if we fail to heed this caution.

Regardless of what happens because of our emotions, we are still held accountable for the consequences. These consequences typically manifest themselves in the other Faces in which we live, and, since we can't escape these consequences, we should at least take responsibility for everything, good or bad, that results from us expressing our emotions. Alexander Pope once said "To err is human, to forgive divine." Forgiveness is always the responsibility of the person who has been slighted, but apologizing is the responsibility of the offender. Because I am speaking directly from my own experience I want to state for the record that I am fully aware that many women have had as rough a childhoods as any man. However, my own conscience has yelled back at me in the midst of depression to say, "Man up!" and tell me to stop blaming everybody else. Many of the tragic circumstances in our childhoods might have been our fathers' faults, but at what point does it become our responsibility to move on? At the risk of getting too personal, I will share an experience I had with my own father to bring home the point.

One of my best friends refers to my dad as "Bill Cosby" because he always seems calm and cool—and he is. But this wasn't always the case. In fact, he was once quite the opposite. Growing up, I remember my father as being a very scary individual, one who was always angry, an alcoholic, and even physically abusive. I specifically remember occasions when I wanted very much for my dad to be proud of my grades or artwork; however, when I approached him, I was consistently turned away brokenhearted, feeling like nothing but a burden. I am sure you can imagine how such treatment could leave a deep scar in a little boy (one that I am sure affects me even now, on some deep, unrecognized level). However, my most painful memories have to do with the interaction between my father and mother. Forever etched in my mind is the horror of watching my dad point a gun at my mother and feeling helpless to do anything about it. Without going into any further detail, I think you get the point. I was unable to forgive my father until I was twenty-one years old. In fact, I didn't have much desire to talk to him at all—ever! It just so happened that I bumped into God and the concept of forgiveness one day. With much reluctance at first, and after many tears, I was able to truly forgive my dad. I remember saying to myself, "Joe, you can either forgive your dad and enjoy some type of relationship with him, or let the anger eat away at you until one day you find yourself wishing you had had more time with him." At that point, I had to make a choice—either allow myself to forgive him or let painful memories deprive me of a father forever. I learned that forgiving my dad was my responsibility—that it could not be dependent on him apologizing for his part in my pain. Once I was able to forgive him, I was able to take responsibility for my own anger, which, in turn, would ultimately prevent me from perpetuating the dysfunction. Emotionally speaking, forgiveness often lies along the road we must travel toward responsibility.

Physical

I am undoubtedly going to hit on a tender subject here, but some things just need to be said. Remember, I am talking from an African American male's perspective, but I believe that all men will be able to relate too much of what I have to say. Ladies, I will attempt to give you something to "shout about" too. I am talking about our physical bodies and how we either maintain or neglect them. Now, for reasons that have nothing to do with the opposite sex, we should take pride in our physical appearance. Too many of us, male and female, are dying from cancers and diseases that are totally preventable by a healthy diet and exercise. Americans are getting bigger and bigger. Obesity in our American youth has reached epidemic proportions. Also, our health can strongly influence our moods and lead to lasting psychological problems. Children are routinely scorned and ridiculed and because of obesity; even adults feel a cold stare or sneer from time to time. Curiously, the biggest abusers of obese people are often themselves, which can perpetuate feelings of depression and self-loathing. I'm not just talking about obesity when I mention health, though—bulimia is just as serious! The images of perfectly formed women and men that are paraded in front of us drive many to extremes, and too often to sickness. We see perfect bodies and come to believe that, somehow, our worth is measured purely by how physically attractive we are to others. Let's be clear—I am not getting down on overweight people or underweight people. What I *am* saying, however, is that if we don't take our physical health seriously enough, then we will likely find ourselves with serious emotional and psychological disorders compounding the physiological ones.

The following generalizations regarding men and women are intended to provide a forum to discuss common behaviors and points of view. I challenge those men and women who do not personally identify with these examples to find parallels in their own lives and meditate on the intent and discovery of such an intrapersonal conversation.

Guys

Beer, TV, fried food, and the couch is a bad combination. If there is anyplace that we set a big double standard, it is in our physical health. We want our women to look eighteen forever! Even more, we want them to overlook the fact that we haven't seen our own toes in quite some time. It's easy for us to reminisce about our six-packs of yesteryear (our guts, not the beer—focus!) and fool ourselves into thinking we are only a few crunches away from the glory days. Just because women have a bigger threshold for tolerating their partners' physical appearance is no reason to constantly require them to endure such tortuous existences. As if the farting, burping, and constant scratching of our unmentionables isn't enough! We have to stop giving them Al Bundy while we ask them for Halle Berry. We need to get off of our collective butts and get rid of our growing guts. Remember the days when we actually played sports instead of just watching them? Okay, so maybe you were never the athletic type—so what? Go to the gym or find someone to play a sport with regularly anyway. The key is to be active in something that we love, or at least develop a workout habit. Wouldn't it be nice to be one of those hunks that your wife or girlfriend dreams about? Do you want her to keep imagining Denzel when she's kissing you? Keeping ourselves in good shape requires a lot of hard work, time management, and, yes, consistent exercise. Personal commitment and a sense of excellence must become a natural part of your daily routine. I'm not suggesting a change in just our thinking, but rather a change in our lifestyle. We must change the way we look at the world if we want to achieve long-term goals. Don't you want to be in your daughter's or son's life a little longer? Then make sure you stay healthy! None of us wants to be a burden to our children as we age, and our best defense is living a healthy life for as long as we can.

Women

I'm sure you had some good laughs while reading the previous section, but now it's your turn. Men and women have some strange perceptions about this thing called love, particularly the concept of unconditional love. For some reason, women seem to think that our concept of love only extends as far as the bedroom. The extent to which a man desires you sexually seems to weigh heavily on your perception of how much he loves you. I know that this is going to sound strange, but many men view these things as mutually exclusive. Contrary to popular belief, a man's mental and emotional state has a lot to do with his level of desire for intimacy in a long-term relationship. However, the level and frequency of intimacy is not a barometer of how much he loves you. If a man truly loves you, then he always will, regardless of your physical makeup. Of course, this in no way means that he will always desire you sexually. Yes, he will go through the motions; it is the need for human affection and physical contact that necessitates this, however, and, before long, it will be clear that his heart just isn't in it (R&B group—Atlantic Starr). I said before to my male readers that we want our women to look eighteen forever—it's selfish, but true. Has it ever occurred to you that we spend most of our lives outside our home seeing beautiful women constantly, only to come home to someone who has taken our affection for granted? I'm not suggesting that women get in full elegance mode for every encounter with her "boo," but what did you do before he committed to you? What hoops did you jump through to keep his attention then? Consider that you show everyone that person we were hot and heavy for all day, then show us a worn-out shell of your former glory at home. This doesn't sound very sensitive, I know. But what can I say? We both must do better.

Are you married with children? Ladies, we understand that you don't lose fat as quickly as men do—it's a scientific fact. We also understand that having children will wreak havoc on your figure. We men like miracles, but don't really expect them in this regard. We do, however, understand that your figure is not a slave to some event that happened years ago. Getting your figure back requires hard work and an internal desire to achieve it. There are no excuses for non-effort! Yes, we need to find better ways of encouraging you, but you have to put in the work. Will we love you if you do nothing? Yes. However, be prepared for the consequences, which often include, but are not limited to, a decreased desire for physical intimacy and affection. It's like putting a TV in your bedroom and thinking that he will be more interested in you with no make-up on and looking like Oprah in *The Color Purple* than in watching ESPN highlights (even though it repeats every half-hour).

In short, we all have challenges when it comes to being physically fit, and it is clearly our own responsibility to maintain our bodies at an acceptable and desirable level of fitness. Sometimes, we get too spiritual and forget that we are also physical beings. *Agape* (unconditional) is the only kind of love that is unconditional—*Eros* is not. No one decides what they become attracted to—it just happens, and we should stop fooling ourselves with unrealistic expectations in our relationships. If we make too many compromises in this area, men and women alike will find difficult to maintain a healthy relationship. Sooner or later, the "real you" always comes out; make sure that you show as much of the real you from the beginning as possible. Reality dictates that old age will compromise and eventually flat-out defy the physical perfection of youth. Take advantage of your youth and fight the effects of age with a healthy lifestyle while you can. Physical attractiveness will almost always be the primary fuel that burns our passions in the beginning—take advantage of it! We will only have personality and spirit to sustain us in our golden years, but Oh! what sweet memories we'll have!

Intellectual

We are physical beings, but our intellect separates us from all other species on the planet. Intellect is not just the ability to learn and reason, it is also the capacity for knowledge and understanding. Humans have a long history that boasts of knowledge far beyond our present-day capacity to understand, which says a lot, considering that we have traveled to the moon, sent probes to far-off planets, and gathered information about places that we will not visit for generations, if ever. We have discovered laws of relativity, quantum mechanics, and physics that both provide information about the universe in which we live and challenge our very belief in creation. We are building devices to create manmade black holes, for crying out loud! Conversely, we can create music, dance, and works of art compelling enough to inspire generations to greatness or destruction. The mind is a terrible thing to waste! We are powerful and weak, strong and frail; our intellects have taken us from fighting with spears to dueling with nuclear warheads. We've learned how to split the atom and proved that our scientific pursuits for power will ultimately have dark outcomes for our enemies. Still, we search for even greater sources of power; we are making headway even as I write these words. Before this generation fades away, we will see technological feats that will blow our collective minds. A mind can be a terrible thing, even if you don't waste it! We cannot allow ourselves to lose respect for God, lest we convince ourselves that we are him.

A recurring theme in this book has been the relationships between men and women. So, I will touch on that perspective as well. Everyone thinks that they are "above average" in one respect or another. Young ladies, we know that you are mature for your age, but not all of you can make that claim. So stay away from the grossly older guys—just because he says that you are mature and had swept you off your feet with deep conversation is no reason to trust him. Men, stop taking advantage of these significantly younger women by using your intellect; it is incredibly irresponsible. Our responsibility, in fact, is to protect our children—even from ourselves, if need be. I know that some women take advantage of young guys too, and that is just as wrong. I suspect, though, that men do it more then women because young women really do mature faster, mentally and physically. After all, not long ago, women used to marry at the tender age of sixteen, and in some states could do so without the permission of their parents. Nuff said!

"Our ability to create beauty is as limitless as our ability to destroy and corrupt it."
From *The Ramblings of Joe Shorter*, 01/10/2006

Spiritual

So, we are emotional, physical, and intellectual beings. What about the spirit? Since the dawn of time, man has worshipped things as varied as other men, rocks, the sun, and The Son. We have prayed to all manner of things, created exhausting rituals, and killed an innumerable number of people all in the name of our gods. If history has taught us anything, it is that there is no atrocity that we will *not* commit in the name of God, nor anything we can achieve higher than that motivated by our belief in God. We are spiritual. We pray and we prey. Cultures across the planet embrace the concept of God and that belief shapes our interactions with each other, either facilitating or straining our ability to coexist. It should seem apparent by now how important it is for us to be mindful of this Face, in which we validate our own existence. Our senses of moral right and wrong depend on what we feel, think, and believe about God.

There is a battle raging within us—the battle of the Faces. We struggle to make a living and to achieve all sorts of things, but no battle is as enduring, exhausting, and overwhelming on our lives as this internal struggle. All of our Faces compete for domination. I have found that the more time I allow my spirit to dominate, the better I am able to deal with the hills and valleys of life. The opposite holds true as well. All of our other Faces are motivated by selfish endeavors, but not the spirit—it is in this way unique. The spiritual part is what longs for goodness, mercy, philanthropy, and selfless acts of sacrifice. It almost seems that I am suggesting that there is no antithesis to the spirit or soul of man. This prompts the question, "What is Evil?" I am only suggesting that the natural inclination of the spirit is good and wholesome because it is with this intent that God created us. However, the other Faces are not by default rooted in goodness; rather, they serve the carnal nature of man. For this reason, our spirit can be corrupted by carnal and self-serving desires, thereby giving rise to an evil spirit or corrupted soul. Christian theology is clear on the idea that Lucifer was the highest-ranking angel in heaven, but let his carnal ambitions and reprobate mind corrupt his sprit, making him the very manifestation of evil itself.

By being mindful of the war that rages within us constantly and by understanding its nature, we can better deal with ebb and flow of the individual skirmishes that are won and lost daily. As people of faith, we should grow to understand that we are ultimately powerless against ourselves, but that it is in this weakness that God can be strong for us. That sounds like a tag-line, but it simply means that it is in our nature to try to control the outcome of everything in our lives. We take on burden after burden in an effort to manipulate our futures. I have learned that if we pick up a burden, God will not force us to put it down. However, we will begin to feel the strain of that burden, and, when our strength fails, we will either drop it or have God take it over for us. We could avoid the fatigue by asking God to hold the brick to begin with. Let's borrow some wisdom from the greatest martial artist of all time, Bruce Lee. Bruce's philosophy centered on the notion that speed, power, and distance seemed to be in natural conflict with one another. He explained that if you can completely relax your muscles and allow all of their power to be focused into your strike, the resulting speed will transmit this power over even very short distances. This concept formed the foundation of his "one-inch punch." In the documentary, "Bruce Lee: The Martial Arts Master" he demonstrated how this approach could knock a man off his feet or split wooden planks. A similar theory can apply to God: if we relax and give over control to God completely, then, when we make a decision, we can do so with incredible power—suddenly! However, if we tense up in anticipation of a fight, we waste energy that could otherwise be used to expand our relationship with Christ, and we consequently need more distance (or time) to generate power (become effective in our lives).

POEM:

Powerful Me

I awake every morning a little dazed and disoriented.
I am first pleasantly surprised that God has given me
another opportunity to change the world on His behalf.

True power is not sought, because there is none to be gained
in the things of this world. Only through God's eternal grace
can power be experienced.

Can I move a mountain? Sure I can—Powerful is God through
me. However, it is not always in the overwhelming miracle acts
that God shows his power; rather, in the "Hello!" given to a
passing stranger. Yes, God knew what that stranger needed
and when, and he chose to do it through a Powerful Me.

A smile, a gesture, a wave of your hand. Through any of these
seemingly small things, future nations can rise and fall, because
your brief presence changed someone's direction or even saved
their life. Now, that person shares his blessing tenfold! Through
God, I can truly be a Powerful Me.

—Joseph William Shorter III
11/06/1999

So how do we become responsible? We make commitments to read and study the
Word of God. We spend time talking to Christ and involving him in every aspect
of our lives. If we find that there is an aspect of our life that is too shameful to
offer that invitation, this is a clear indication that we should expend energy in
removing that aspect, or at least abstain from the behavior. If this walk were easy,
what would be the great reward for doing so? Giving up control doesn't mean
that we will no longer endure hardships and heartache; rather, it affords us the
ability handle it better. You and I have heard a billion times that "prayer changes
things." I believe that wholeheartedly. However, I believe the change is mostly
inside ourselves, as opposed to a change that violates someone else's free will. Let
me elaborate.

Scenario

*Disclaimer: this is a fictitious story, but someone reading may have had this
exact experience.

Hypothetically, a man works for an individual who has nothing but contempt for
him, but his boss remained powerless to fire him because he lacks valid cause.
Every day, he has to deal with ugly attitudes, abide by newly created rules that
seem to apply just to him, and basically work in a hostile environment. Since no

pleas to upper management or human resources have yielded any results, He began to pray for both his supervisor and for his ability to represent God in such a taxing environment. Eventually, his boss experiences a major tragedy in his life and finds comforting words sparing among so-called friends and relatives. Knowing that his employee attended church regularly, the supervisor turns to him and asks him to pray for him and his family.

In the scenario above, I believe that prayer did change things. It has changed the employee. Prayer allowed him to let the fruits of the spirit shine through; it prevented him from reveling in his supervisor's pain, and enabled another lost soul to see a physical representation of Christ.

Well, then, what of the supernatural changes that have been accredited to prayer? As long as it does not violate the idea of free will, God will and can perform miracles for his own glory, not ours. Remember, God gave us free will to enable us to choose him. He will not make us choose him if we don't of our own accord. Free will also makes it clear that we are responsible for the choices we make; although God is just and faithful, and forgives us our trespasses, this does not mean that we will escape the consequences of our own actions.

POEM:

God's Way

When you awake in the morning and your day begins,
Do you think of work, or maybe calling a friend?
Or do you fall to your knees and begin to pray?
When you started, did you do it yours, or God's way?

While on your way to work, you see the traffic is insane,
And a car cuts you off while trying to merge into your lane.
Do you curse, make obscene gestures, and become hateful?
Or do you praise GOD for protecting you both and being faithful?
So what did you do when some stranger almost ruined your day?
Did you respond yours, or God's way?

As you entered your office and things were all confused,
Your boss screaming in one ear and you want to blow a fuse.

Do you raise your voice and reply with a tone that can kill?
Or do you find HIS peace—STAND and be still?
So how did you respond, and what did you say?
Did you do it yours, or God's way?

Now it's time to go home, and no progress seemingly made.
Your head has been pounding, and you are due a raise.
When someone says "Good night," is your response nice or rude?
Do you shake your head in disgust and let stress overtake your mood?
Or will you remember to count it all Joy and find rest in HIM every day?
So tell me, what did you do, and was it yours or God's way?

—Joseph William Shorter III
01/06/2000

Chapter 5
Self-Profiling

Who am I, and what is my purpose? Wow! What great questions! These are undoubtedly two of the most common asked by all humans. In the previous chapter, I laid out the idea that our spiritual beliefs help frame the context in which we can answer these and many other questions. Self-profiling is more than asking ourselves a bunch of questions. The answers and the subsequent evaluation of the answers is where the meaning and usefulness come from. In my perspective, we should ask, seek to answer, and evaluate the answer and its impact on how we live and operate in the world around us as often as we can. Life is a process, not an event. The sum total of our lives will be far greater than we can ever imagine.

"Let the impression you leave on the world be the legacy you leave for it."
From *The Ramblings of Joseph Shorter,* 11/21/2005

Intrapersonal Examination

Personally, this continual process has led to more new questions and to fewer answers than I'd like, but the process of seeking the answers continues to be invaluable. Inevitably, a person begins to ask more specific questions. We also begin to cast more self-righteous judgments on others. Do any of the following remarks sound like they could have come from you?

- What would I do in that situation?

- Why doesn't anyone understand my pain?

- I can't believe that he/she could do that!

- Why do I not feel more pain after this loss?

- I can't believe she got an abortion; I would never do that!

It seems to me that it is a very rare thing for people to have original thoughts. Not only does this sound weird, it requires more explanation, so I will do so by sharing a personal moment. Shortly after forgiving my dad for his part in my difficult childhood, I found myself engaged in intellectual conversation with him at his house in Atlanta. First, let me say that my mom and dad are two of the smartest people I know, so this mental exercise with my father was particularly enjoyable. The thing that stands out, even to this day, is a specific question my dad asked me: "What is nothing?" Immediately, I began to speak words that closely resemble what you might find in any dictionary (see below). Soon, I began to realize that it couldn't *really* be defined, because any definition was, in fact, something. What happened next was eye-opening. For the first time that I was aware of, I had an original thought process. Most of the time, I hadn't questioned much in my life. I was a Christian because my family was, not because of some personal experience. In fact, most of my life followed that pattern. So that conversation kick-started the intellectual pursuits that would follow.

Nothing:
Something that has no existence. Something that has no quantitative value; zero: a score of two to nothing. One that has no substance or importance; a nonentity: "A nothing is a dreadful thing to hold onto." (Edna O'Brien). **Source:** *http://dictionary.reference.com/browse/Nothing*

Therefore, I encourage you to take an inward look and ask yourself whether your beliefs were handed to you or have been arrived at by way of your own thought processes. This is important in determining who you really are (today), and what you really feel. I have found that debating certain positions aloud with other people helps to either solidify my position or to change it. I will admit my pride does not always allow me to confess to the person or people I am talking with that I have changed my position; however, it does happen from time to time. In fact, I will often use the argument that convinced me to later persuade someone else.

Self-Righteousness

We often project unrealistic expectations on others and the situations or circumstances in their lives. We, too, become victims of the same scrutiny that we so readily apply to others, but we always seem to have excuses for our faults. We all share common emotions. There is nothing new under the sun, and this includes a particular emotion or scenario that *you* might think is unique. All of us are dishonest to some extent with our friends, family, associates—and especially ourselves. This dishonesty is part of a natural self-defense mechanism we all share. It has been said that honesty is the best policy, but I don't think many of us really believe it when it comes to the skeletons in our own closets.

At the core, we are trying to determine our nature. "Am I essentially a good or bad person?" The question is usually rigged, because no one (generally speaking) wants to live with the realization that they are a "bad" person, unless, of course, they are in the throes of a pity-party. So, we reason away most of our guilt—when you think about it, what else are we to do? We, above all others, must either live with ourselves or end our own lives because the weight of the guilt and pressure is overwhelming. Usually, we find a way to cope. Have you ever noticed how easy it is for us to pardon someone else's transgressions when we have committed the same offence? (As long as, of course, we ourselves are not the victims of the injustice.) We rationalize our shortcomings and bad decisions so that we can function in a world that we fear Will burn us at the stake if only they knew our dark secrets.

Looking at ourselves with such a raw perspective can help us to become much more accepting of others and their faults and much better at forgiving people who have offended us in some fashion. The best way to recognize that our own breath smells is to have someone else tell us, even though it's also the most embarrassing way. This is what Jesus does for us when we cultivate a relationship with him. Knowing Jesus will subsequently cause us to have more compassion. Our hidden darkness, after all, is not hidden to Jesus; the fact that he would sacrifice so much for a wretch like me makes it clear that I shouldn't cast judgment on others. This is not to say that you couldn't or shouldn't tell someone of their halitosis problem—tactfully. For these and other reasons, we should seek to uncover ourselves, so that we aren't wasting energy trying to be a different person to everybody we meet. You would be surprised at how much can be learned about other people's decisions through looking at how you handle your own.

Exercise 1

- Make a list of all the beliefs that you have today. Some examples are; I am a _____ (religion), political affiliation, stance on interracial dating or marriage, etc.

- Write a position paper about how you feel about each belief. The position paper should be at least one page long (double-spaced).

- Pick one (or all) of them, and have a discussion with a friend about what they think about the topic.

Why do this? Because it is important that you know more than anyone else about what you believe, or think you believe. The lives we live seem so very complicated, don't they? We live in so many dimensions that I think we confuse ourselves and forget who we are supposed to be, and we often base our responses on who is seeing us right now.

POEM:

Living in Three Dimensions

What is it that **we see** of others' lives that make us envious? Do we not know that the painting we see is made up of a multitude of conflicting strokes? "Oh, they are meant to be," and "They look so cute together," are the whispers of the patrons attending the Broadway show. However, is what we see really what we know?

What is it that **we feel** as actors in a play? How disturbing is it to find out that we participated in writing, directing, and producing every laugh, cry, and hope today. Could it be that simple? Sure, but there is a catch. We write the scripts of our lives in permanent ink, so consequences must follow what can't be taken back. However, ours is the only character that is controlled with the ink of our thoughts. Happy, sad, content, distraught—take care, for we will reap what we wrought.

What we dream is hidden in the corners of our hearts.
We must let our dreams be made not of what we see or feel in our everyday walk. Rather, they should be the sum of visions of possibilities stitched in the fabric gossamer thoughts.

It is in the genius of our greatest achievements and the sin of our lowest lows that we make our mark. Will we be remembered for our mistakes or our greatness? Our being is but a struggle of life that shapes our environment, our ups and our downs. Our memory will be worn on those we affect with faces adorned with smiles or frowns.

—Joseph W. Shorter III
03/02/2005

Exercise 2

- Write down your dreams and categorize whether you think they are achievable or not.

- Explain why they can be achieved or not.

- Make a fictitious plan to achieve them.

- Try to apply the plan a little each day, just in case it's not so impossible after all.

*Note—It might help to think about what you would do if money weren't an issue.

Exercise 3

- Write down all the things that you don't like to do.

- Explain in detail why, and categorize them by things you used to like as a child, things you haven't tried, and things you have tried and have never liked.

- Try at least one new thing not on any list and add it to the list in the proper category if you don't like it each month.

Exercise 4

- Write down all of the things you think you are good at and give an example of each one.

- Write down all of the things you think you are bad at and give an example of each one.

- Summarize how you think your personality contributes to these strengths and weaknesses.

"We all struggle to overcome our weaknesses. However, it is the wisest of us who understands the inherent weakness in every strength and the inherent strength in every weakness. Mastering this should be our goal."
Joseph W. Shorter 01/04/2006

Chapter 6

The Emotional Underverse

Simply put, these are the emotions underneath one's emotions. You see, it is rare that the origin of a person's emotional response is directly related to the issue at hand. You should understand that I am not a psychologist, nor do I intend to postulate on varying clinical definitions of emotion. In fact, this entire book is but an opinion. It is my hope to raise in you the awareness of a world of emotions that exists on a semi-subconscious level that we are not always aware of. There are many published discussions, papers, and theories regarding emotion, from the works of Descartes to publications by Oxford University Press, Cambridge University Press, and similar well-respected publishers. As always, it helps to give examples that help to illustrate my point. As I have grown older, I have been better able to identify suitable approaches to handling situations in my life that have been directly influenced by my parents.

How I manage my depression, for example, parallels how my mother copes with hers. We hold our feelings in and try not to expose people to our emotional whims because, well, it just isn't polite. Instead, we try to deal with problems by internalizing our anger and disappointment. Unfortunately, we don't learn easily from our past mistakes and find ourselves continually disappointed by how inconsiderate other people seem to be regarding our feelings. We instead rediscover, time and again, that our priorities are not as much a concern for others as they expect their priorities to be for us. My mother is an incredibly strong individual; her compassion for others causes her to be self-sacrificing, at times to a fault. I share this characteristic with my mother, and, while it is noble, it can be damaging because of the resulting exposure to hurt and pain; ultimately, it contributes to our depression. Ironically, we find it hard to allow ourselves to be cared for because we don't want to be a burden; therefore, we try to shield others and ourselves from our needs. Subsequently, we struggle to find balance in trusting and giving in all our relationships. We are usually the ones who get left behind while the bus of caring and healing speeds away because either no one knew we were hurting (waiting for the bus) or we were too scared to pay the fare. As I was growing up, my mother quickly became my hero, and she remains so today. There seemed to be nothing my mother couldn't do. She has always been intelligent and resourceful, and a determination seemed to perennially adorn her stature. She has always been strong for her children, and she has worked hard to hide her pain and depression. Later in life, I discovered that my mom is a manic-depressive and struggles silently to balance her emotions. She has been a super wife, a super mom—a superwoman. Although my mom was obviously conflicted when I was growing up, she always managed to remain loving and supportive enough to make up for the dysfunctional relationship we all had with my father.

I now struggle (even while writing this book) with the same dynamic my mother struggled with. Learning to deal with this in a healthy manner is an ongoing process, but recognizing the connection helps with the daily effort. While you, the reader, may find your own personal connection to your mother to be a little different, I hope this example helps to illustrate my point that we must look beyond the surface of our reactions and deeper to discover the source of our responses.

I used to think that, because of my difficult childhood, I got nothing of value from my father, but I eventually learned otherwise. Sometimes, it is clear that my father's name isn't the only thing that I got from him. In some ways, we are exactly alike! My father is incredibly smart, and sometimes I believe that this intellect leads him to be eccentric at times. My dad and I can be passionately expressive, yet, paradoxically, we often struggle to communicate feelings and emotions honestly. We both seem to fight a constant struggle between the idealistic and the logical. It is this dichotomy that makes our emotions treacherous waters for those brave souls who get involved with us. For it is not just the waves of passion that one needs to be worried about, but also the passing undercurrents. Instinctively, we search for the hidden meanings and motives behind everything we deal with, sizing them up and categorizing them while trying to decide, like a chess player, what our next ten moves will be. As if that isn't complicated enough, both of our distressed childhoods have contributed to our difficulties in exposing our feelings to loved ones. Although my dad has not shared this with me specifically, I believe that he experiences emotions even more deeply and more powerfully than I do. The trust required to expose emotions must have been violated by someone extremely close to him long ago. The memory of the pain rules our willingness to allow anyone else that type of access to our hearts. So we deal with life, emotionally speaking, always at arm's length, longing for that closeness that we can only allow for short durations because we feel that we will inevitably be violated again.

It might sound like some of the things that I have described regarding my parents are weaknesses or "bad" tendencies, but they're not. Of course, these aren't the only things that I share with them, but that discussion is for another time. The very emotional characteristics I have discussed are strengths and weakness at the same time. As I begin to understand the origin of my emotions and how they influence my decisions, it makes sense that, sometimes, some of my decisions confuse me. I am now better able to balance and draw on the strength related to the characteristics more often than I fall victim to the weakness in them. I am surely not unlike many of you reading this book. I believe that we all have conflicting currents of emotions that swell within us. Some of the emotions crash violently against the waves of life, while others erupt in underwater volcanoes and earthquakes that are hardly detected on the surface. Unfortunately, sometimes those underwater catastrophes cause tsunamis that inflict damage on whoever is unable to see them coming. We must strive to find techniques to uncover and deal with the sources of these disasters in our lives. Here are some good questions that might help to uncover the layers:

- Why do I sabotage relationships when I find happiness in them?

- Why is it so hard for me to articulate to others what I feel?

- What unhealthy behaviors do I bring to my job, relationships, etc.?

- Do I truly believe that I deserve to be happy?

- Do I truly believe that the bliss of true love is even obtainable? If not, is my doubt the result of the relationship my mother and father shared?

Personally, I have struggled with the question of deserving happiness. I look at the pain I have needlessly and carelessly inflicted on others and wonder why I should ever find contentment. Sometimes, I wonder whether any joy I may bring into someone's life is worth the pain I fear loving me will eventually bring. All of these conflicting emotions come from deep within and take time to work out. Fear prevents us from opening up our junky closets—we are unsure of how to protect ourselves from the falling debris that awaits our curiosity.

How do we cope?

I imagine that most of us cope through a combination of therapy and denial. Therapy comes in many forms. It could be a friend that you have grown comfortable enough with to share a specific part of your Underverse. It could be your wife or husband who helps you navigate your emotional seas. Simply put, therapy can be anything that allows you to work out the destructive part of your emotions safely and over a period of time. Since emotions can be extremely powerful, we must take care in how and to whom we expose them. It is easier to talk to someone whose judgment cannot affect your life directly—in other words, in an environment in which it is safe to show your bad side. Most of us hide behind a veil because we don't want to risk losing relationships by being too honest. "If they knew, how could they hold me in high esteem ever again?" And it is their esteem that we covet so much. We validate ourselves through others' opinions of us more than we like to admit, so complete openness is always a slippery slope. However, the relaxation and comfort in being able to be transparent with someone else is invaluable. We all want someone to know everything about us—the good and the bad—and still love and accept us. We seek this acceptance in people all the time, but accept only parts of it from different people. This hole we feel is never filled, because only God can love us completely, yet we fight against him, too. The more we examine ourselves, the more we will find that *we* are the source of conflict, not the world around us.

Of course, we could just deny that anything or anyone shapes our character, failings, achievements, and so on. We could go on finding temporary substitutes for the fulfillment we lack in various parts of our lives. A lot of people use sex, sports, alcohol, TV, shopping, friendships, pampering, and religiosity to fill this same void created by the failure to face the origins and root causes of emotional issues. Scientifically speaking, it is understandable why atheists believe that God is nothing but a construct of our minds—the one person who cannot fall short of our expectations and who loves us no matter what. For the record, I reject this notion altogether because of my personal belief that God—and subsequently Christ—provides us with an example of how we should love and treat each other in every relationship between imperfect people. I believe that God is the creator of all and is perfect in all. It is our struggle to walk the road that leads us closer to God, but God has promised to help us if we accept his gift of sacrifice. What can we do, then? Try these tips:

- Pray.

- Study the word of God by attending a church regularly and by taking advantage of educational opportunities provided by the church.

- Spend time working out your difficulties with Christ more than you try to do so with men and women.

- Spend more time with yourself.

POEM:

GOD Is There

Stand tall, lift your head up!
child of GOD, salt of the Earth.

Winds may blow,
nations will fall, but GOD's
love for you endureth it all!

He gave us his Son, glory full and bold
cleansed of all sin,
from small child to very old!

His joy is our stronghold,
our sword our shield.
The armor of GOD,
his battles—stand and fight
We will!

Never lose faith in our Father above,
his word is Truth, a ROCK, never removed.
Stand on it, be secure,
his word He'll prove.

So in conclusion don't become disillusioned, for GOD is there.
Through good, through bad—your deepest despair.

So when he brings you out of the storm and the weather is fair.
Forget not whence cometh your help,

high in the clouds and in your heart—
GOD is there!

—Joseph William Shorter III
12/09/1999

Chapter 7
Walking in Power

Identifying Sources of Power

Family can be one of the things that helps to anchor us in society. Those of you who enjoyed a happy and well-balanced childhood know that you often draw on the stability of those experiences as a guide to finding your place in the world—from the memories of Grandma's unbeatable apple pie to the assurance that dad would always come home and shower you with the significance all little children crave. Childhood memories are powerful and are often the basis for most of our aspirations in life. These pleasant memories are the very examples that we seek to duplicate in our own relationships. Not all of us had stable and well-adjusted childhoods that we can now draw from, but good and bad childhood experiences alike weigh heavy on how we view the world, our place in it, and purpose for it. Negative situations are also powerful motivators, so it is up to us to use whatever family relationships we have had to springboard ourselves toward positive and meaningful pursuits.

Friends

"Friendship" is a word that has probably been misused as much or more than the word "love." We are introduced to the concept of friendship early in life through interactions with our parents' friends' children, neighborhood kids, and schoolmates. It is only through our experiences that we become aware of the confusion of determining what makes a true friend. Whether it is through our own selfish betrayal of those we called friends or vice versa, it becomes clear that friendship is more than an association with someone who just happened to share the same neighborhood or school as we did. Soon, we categorize people into neat subclasses of friendship—associates, acquaintances, buddies, colleagues, and so on. Soon, we have to make a distinction between friend and true friend because we realize that the latter designation can only be given without reservation after adversity and pain.

"The best thing a Friend can be is Available"

We find that true friends are those who aren't afraid of losing us because they tell the truth even when it may bruise our egos. Friends are the shelters we seek in the storms of our lives. They are safe havens in those times when our bad decisions demand retribution and we feel like outcasts. These are the people we trust; their motivations are not in question, nor do they conflict with our well-being. We invite these privileged few into the inner chambers of our life because they won't summarily judge us as bad people. We love our friends because they love us despite our faults. We can and do tap into this power frequently. Choose your friends wisely and be careful not to abuse them or allow them to abuse you. If you can do this, those four or five lifetime friends will help make life more livable and enjoyable, especially in old age.

Community

"It takes a neighborhood to raise a child" used to be one of our national mottoes, but not anymore. When I was younger, if I got a whipping at school, then I was in for a killing at home. Any adult in the community had unspoken permission to discipline me—that was just how it was. We always knew that our parents had eyes everywhere, and news of our wrongdoings traveled back home faster than we could. However, if, for some reason, we didn't encounter punishment at the front door, we would lose sleep every night until we felt the cold sting of a belt, switch, or whatever else was handy. Conversely, the entire community often celebrated achievement making one feel like a hero at times. Unfortunately, it seems our sense of community has dwindled to all but nothing. Parents and adults don't know whether to be more afraid of child-protection agencies or the children themselves. There are still communities and small towns around that retain this old-school approach, and we could learn much from them. It is more likely, though, that we don't know more than four families in the gated communities we live in. We even pay more for homes with gates that give us a false sense of security. What happened to the times when we could sleep with our doors unlocked? In fact, a large number of thieves and vandals come from within our own gates, disguised as undisciplined children playing in the street. The good news is that it is not too late to build a stronger sense of community and still enjoy the level of privacy that we have grown accustomed to. Concerned parents and residents still have the power to build neighborhood-watch programs and to watch out for sex offenders moving into or prowling the area. There is strength in reaching out to and connecting with the people who live around you.

Suggested readings and information:

Holy Bible:
http://www.biblegateway.com/
John 3:16 (King James Version)
For God so loved the world, that he gave his only begotten Son, that whosoever believeth in him should not perish, but have everlasting life.

Romans 10:9 (King James Version)
That if thou shalt confess with thy mouth the Lord Jesus, and shalt believe in thine heart that God hath raised him from the dead, thou shalt be saved.

John 1:1, 14 (King James Version)
In the beginning was the Word, and the Word was with God, and the Word was God.
…
And the Word was made flesh, and dwelt among us, (and we beheld his glory, the glory as of the only begotten of the Father,) full of grace and truth.

Talking the Talk

We need to begin changing our daily language, and this starts with renewing our minds. If we think differently, those new thoughts will change our language. Do you have one of those friends whose conversation seems to be always negative? Are *you* one of those friends? You might have noticed that before they call, you might be in a good mood, but three seconds into the conversation you somehow become as cynical as they are. Most of us seem to gravitate to negative thinking more easily than to positive thinking, and this tendency helps to reinforce our feelings of helplessness and despair. Once we get into a funk, we help ourselves stay there by focusing on the problem instead of the solution. Sometimes, the consequences of our choices seem so overwhelming that we can't fathom surviving them. Soon, this somber outlook shows up in our body language. We walk the halls staring at the ground with long faces and eating the fattening cookies that we look like someone has stolen from us.

Instead, we should focus on the positive things that emerge from our trials and tribulations—like the fact that we have survived them. Not only that, we will also learn from them, and these lessons will serve as testimonies for the people we meet later in life who might be having similar struggles. We so often think that our problems only affect *us,* which is a short-sighted view of most of what really happens. How we respond will invariably affect the people we interact with. If you are a leader at work, then be careful about how you start the day, because others will feed off your energy like a baby in a mother's womb. Thessalonians 5:17 tells us to pray without ceasing. This is good advice, because it will help us focus on God and his goodness. Keep this type of focus throughout your day, then notice how different the outcome is—not just for you, but for everyone around you too.

Walking the Walk

It isn't good enough to talk a good game—we must also work on *living* one. It is interesting to see how we approach our lives when it comes to improving our attitudes. I suspect that we don't really come up with a solid game plan or set goals with deadlines that help us evaluate our own progress. No, I would venture to say that most of us handle this much in the same way we do our New Year's resolutions—we start out strong for the first week, the second week we begin to wonder what the big deal is, anyway, and by the third week, we have convinced ourselves that we're beautiful just the way we are. Well, how, then, will tomorrow be any different if we do the same thing we did yesterday? This walk is much too hard to maintain over any real length of time (like the rest of our lives) without help. This is where the true friends I mentioned earlier can help. You need an accountability partner, and maybe more than one. You need someone to whom you have given permission to get on your case about otherwise taboo subjects. Also, it is not a good idea for you to be their accountability partner in return, because we all have a tendency to deflect and attack when we are being criticized. So, if you are looking for someone to criticize so that you can feel better about yourself, then you are missing the point.

I saw an interview with Jean-Claude Van Damme some time ago, and he said something that I have always remembered: "I used to imagine myself being a cool guy that everyone wanted to be, so one day I started pretending that I was that guy. Before I knew it, I was that guy." It's important not to bite off more than you can chew—just start to pretend that you are happy, cool, or any other positive thing you want to be, and start doing the things that can make it possible. Sooner or later, you might just be that person you wish you were, and then you can stop pretending.

Conclusion

Rediscovering African American Wisdom is an effort to shock many back into consciousness. We are all more similar to each other than we are different. So look at yourself in the mirror and consider the points and perspectives that were discussed earlier. It is not enough that we are mad, we must know *why*. It is not enough that we just exist—we must *live*. Everyone has the potential to improve their life through introspection, and the intent of this book has been to start you on that path. The only person we can blame for our underachievement is ourselves, and, ironically, we hold all the power of success inside ourselves as well. God has given us example after example, as well as a guidebook for our journey through life. Life isn't long enough to linger in a regretful past. When we forgive ourselves, we can forgive others and truly move on.

I sincerely hope that this book has helped shed light on a perspective that you might not have seen before. I sincerely thank you for taking the time to read it. Many people and conversations have contributed to my perspectives on all of the issues I have mentioned. I pray that you, too, develop your own unique perspective, and that the insights you pass on bless someone else's life.

Resources, Research & Suggested Readings

1. U.S. Constitution
   http://www.archives.gov/national-archives-experience/charters/constitution.html

2. Studies in Emotion
   http://plato.stanford.edu/entries/emotion/

3. Blue Letter Bible—Hebrew & Greek translation tool
   http://www.blueletterbible.org/

4. Bible Gateway
   http://www.biblegateway.com/passage/

5. The Afro-American Almanac
   http://www.toptags.com/aama

   - This is a incredible site. It has vast African American resources and information. There are even books that you can read directly on the Web site.

6. Books

   - *Black Heroes* by Jesse Carney Smith
   - *Uncle Tom's Cabin* by Harriet Beecher Stowe
   - *Reconstruction* by Frederick Douglass and various others
   - *The Case of the Negro* by Booker T. Washington
   - *When You Don't Know What To Do* by Rev. Arthur T. Jones

Ten Commandments: http://www.mechon-mamre.org/p/pt/pt0220.htm#2

Answers to Pop Quiz

- Without looking it up, write down the Ten Commandments.

  - Exodus 20:2-17 paraphrased

    1. You shall have no other gods before me

    2. You shall not take the name of God in vain

    3. Keep the Sabbath holy

    4. Honor thy father and mother

    5. You shall not kill

    6. You shall not commit adultery

    7. You shall not steal

    8. You shall not bear false witness against thy neighbor

    9. You shall not covet thy neighbor's house

    10. You shall not covet thy neighbor's wife, nor anything that is thy neighbor's http://www.mechon-mamre.org/p/pt/pt0220.htm#2

- What is the capital of the state that you live in right now?

  - Tallahassee, Florida

- What countries border Iraq?

  - Syria, Iran, Saudi Arabia, Kuwait, Jordan, Turkey
    http://www.mideastweb.org/maps.htm

- Name ten countries in Africa.

  Algeria, Angola, Benin, Botswana, Burkina Faso, Burundi, Cameroon, Cape Verde, Central African Republic, Chad, Comoros, Republic of Congo, Democratic Republic of The Congo, Cote d'Ivoire, Djibouti, Egypt, Equatorial Guinea, Eritrea, Ethiopia, Gabon, The Gambia, Ghana, Guinea, Guinea-Bissau, Ivory Coast (Cote d'Ivoire), Kenya, Lesotho, Liberia, Libya, Madagascar, Malawi, Mali, Mauritania, Mauritius, Morocco, Mozambique, Namibia, Niger, Nigeria, Rwanda, Sao Tome and Principe, Senegal, Seychelles, Sierra Leone, Somalia, South Africa, Sudan, Swaziland, Tanzania, Togo, Tunisia, Uganda, Zambia, Zimbabwe

Source: http://www.library.northwestern.edu/africana/map/
Source: http://geography.about.com/library/maps/blrafrica.htm

- Name five significant black heroes, aside from Martin Luther King Jr., Malcolm X, and Frederick Douglass.

    - Booker T. Washington
      http://www.gale.com/free_resources/bhm/bio/washington_b.htm

    - Marcus Garvey
      http://www.marcusgarvey.com/wmview.php?ArtID=531

    - Carter G. Woodson
      http://www.marcusgarvey.com/wmview.php?ArtID=516

    - Queen Makeda of Sheba
      http://www.marcusgarvey.com/wmview.php?ArtID=478

    - Zenobia, Warrior Queen of the East
      http://www.marcusgarvey.com/wmview.php?ArtID=461

- Without looking it up, what is the Fifteenth Amendment to the U.S. Constitution about?

    - The right to vote regardless of color. (It gave black men the right to vote.)
      http://www.law.cornell.edu/constitution/constitution.amendmentxv.html

- Do you have a family tree? Yes or No.

    - Good resource to start:
      http://www.ancestry.com/?o_xid=21852&o_lid=21852

- What part of the country is Wyoming in?

    - The Mountain States
      Source:
      http://www.hipark.austin.isd.tenet.edu/projects/fifth/states/home.html

- Who was the sixteenth president of the United States?

- Abraham Lincoln
  http://www.whitehouse.gov/history/presidents/al16.html

- Name three influential people of the Harlem Renaissance.

  - Langston Hughes—http://www.poets.org/poet.php/prmPID/83

  - Claude McKay—http://www.spartacus.schoolnet.co.uk/ARTmckay.htm

  - Countee Cullen—
    http://www.english.uiuc.edu/maps/poets/a_f/cullen/cullen.htm

  - Zora Neale Hurston—
    http://www-hsc.usc.edu/~gallaher/hurston/hurston.html

  - Nella Larsen—
    http://www.library.csi.cuny.edu/dept/history/lavender/386/nlarsen.html

About The Author

I was born on August 1, 1970, in Maricopa County in Phoenix, Arizona to Joseph William Shorter II and Laura Hill Shorter. When I was only one year old, my family packed up everything and moved across the country to Greensboro, North Carolina, where our perfect American family seemed to take root. Soon after, however, we moved to Louisville, Kentucky, because of my father's job relocation, and our paradise was then interrupted by the arrival of five brothers and sisters previously unknown to my sister and me. It was then that my real education in life began. A broken home and a seared childhood would 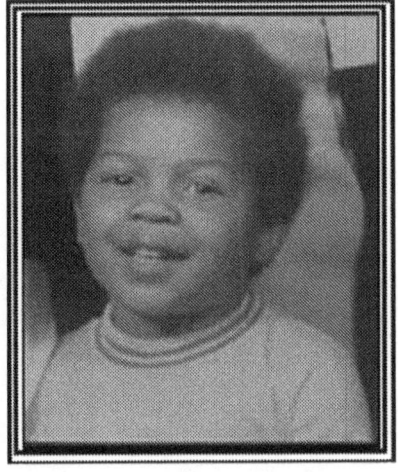 be my reality. My mom and dad divorced when I was ten, and the struggle continued from there. I graduated from Southside High School, but not before fathering my own son, Brandon, when I was seventeen. Between work and high school, my grades sank low enough to encourage me to enter the U.S. Marine Corps Reserves in the fall of 1988. After my return from boot camp and Military Occupational Specialty training school, I returned home with few options. I then scrounged out a living working at McDonald's and living with my mom until I decided that a grown man should be self-sufficient. This revelation earned me a six-month homeless stint before my pride allowed me to accept the extended hand of my friend David Cross, who invited me to be his roommate along with another friend, Jeff Horton. Eventually, I ran my own cleaning business until I was able to increase my participation in the military to full-time service, which I continued for nine years. During this period, I married my first wife, Shawn Carter, and we had a child, Jasmine Shorter, on December 7, 1996. I currently live in Tampa, Florida, where I am a software developer and am married to my best friend Constance S. Blaize-Shorter.

978-0-595-40702-6
0-595-40702-1

www.ingramcontent.com/pod-product-compliance
Lightning Source LLC
Chambersburg PA
CBHW020340290526
45785CB00005B/2107